The QPB Companion to
Shakespeare

Quality Paperback Book Club
New York

Copyright © 2002 by Bookspan. All rights reserved.

Acknowledgment of permission to reprint previously copyrighted material can be found on page 94.

The QPB Companion to Shakespeare is a publication of Quality Paperback Book Club, 1271 Avenue of the Americas, New York, NY 10020.

Edited by Brandon Geist

Book design by Christos Peterson

ISBN: 1-58288-037-9

Printed in the United States of America

Contents

INTRODUCTION
by Brandon Geist

I have to admit that I first set upon editing this Companion with a certain lack of enthusiasm, because, well, I'm a little sick of Shakespeare. As a kid I read his plays and poems with the sort of eagerness generally reserved for after-school cartoons or plastic toy soldiers (yes, believe it or not, before I was an editor at QPB, I was a little nerd). On various summer evenings, I was taken by my parents, eager to fill my precocious young mind with Elizabethan verse, to performances of Shakespeare in a park—not *The* Park, mind you, but *a* park . . . in suburban Pennsylvania. Later as a teenager, a group of friends and I put on our own production of *A Midsummer Night's Dream* and guilted our friends and family into paying good money to watch us butcher a literary classic. I would later build on this experience by entering a Shakespearean monologue competition, somehow making it to the national level, wherest I got to butcher a classic monologue in Lincoln Center before a panel of judges, whilst pterodactyl-sized butterflies reenacted the Jurassic Period inside my stomach. Perhaps this adventure more than any other compelled me to take the prolonged hiatus from the Shakespeare canon that I was enjoying before I sat down to put together this little volume.

But as I began to research and revisit my literary friend of adolescence, I began to rediscover what I had enjoyed so much in Shakespeare—first, his wit and second, his wisdom. Shakespeare once quipped in *Twelfth Night*: "Better a witty fool than a foolish wit." Shakespeare betters both. His works sparkle with a love of language and a love of life. His words compel us to read with eyes alert to every letter and every space between every letter, and to listen with ears pricked up, twitching like those of a cat on the prowl, tracking down elusive wordplays and puns darting by. But Shakespeare is no "foolish wit"—even the most frolicsome of his comedies is a meditation on human nature, poised not just to tickle our funny bones and challenge our verbal cunning but to challenge our very way of being. Enjoying Shakespeare not only requires a certain level of intelligence, enjoying Shakespeare makes us more intelligent and possibly, wiser. Perhaps this is the reason why Shakespeare is still so vital, relevant, and at time almost sickeningly ubiquitous—because even now, four hundred-some years later, nobody is all that much wiser. We still need to read our Shakespeare.

People definitely are still reading their Shakespeare—the problem is that some of them are reading Shakespeare where Shakespeare isn't. In 1995 Donald Foster, a professor of English at Vassar famous as a literary sleuth after he unmasked Joe Klein as the author of *Primary Colors*, made an astonishing case that Shakespeare was the author of a little-known 578-line poem called "A Funeral Elegy." As a result of Foster's pronouncement, the poem was added to three major editions of Shakespeare's work and Harold Bloom even included it in his chronology of Shakespeare's writing in his acclaimed book *Shakespeare: The Invention of the Human*. This summer Foster admitted that he was wrong, and so the poem has been shot like missile out of the canon. The currently prevailing theory, put forth by Gilles D. Monsarrat, a professor of languages at the University of Burgundy in France, is that the author of the elegy was actually John Ford (1586-1640), a writer best known for dramatic works like *'Tis Pity She's a Whore*. Even in 2002, Shakespeare continues to intrigue and beguile. (If you want to read the poem in question, go no further than the end of this Introduction, where the elegy is handily attached.)

So the question "What the heck did Shakespeare actually write?" does come up occasionally, but a much more common question is "Who was this William Shakespeare?" This puzzle has haunted scholars and readers for centuries. In the first section of this Companion, "The Man," (entitled so because, well, Shakespeare is the man) we take a brief look at the embittered authorship controversy—where do you fall: Stratfordian or Oxfordian or like me, completely indifferent-ian? Addressing the more metaphysical question of Shakespeare's identity, we take a look, of course, at what he himself read—because being ourselves the squirmiest of bookworms, we can't help but think that we are what we read and so the best way to know Shakespeare the man must be to know what texts Shakespeare the man consumed. And speaking of Shakespeare as a man, we cannot ignore the question of his sexual orientation, because let's face it, even in these most tolerant of times, the people still want to know "Was Shakespeare Gay?"

But enough gossip. One thing we know for sure about Shakespeare—he had a way with words, such a way that we're all quoting him on an almost daily basis, often without even knowing it. In the second section, "The Words," we look at Will's impact upon the English language—the playwright and poet coined phraseology ranging from "dead as a doornail" to "hoodwinked" to "neither rhyme nor reason." And then just to make sure the first section isn't the only one that mentions sex, we take a gander at the impact of Elizabethan English on the bard's bawdy passages (of which there are many) in our "Glossary of Sexual Slang" in the Shakespearean canon.

In the next segment, "The Critics," we meet two men who've read so much Shakespeare, both the dirty and not-so-dirty bits, that they'd have little need for such a glossary. The (in)famous literary critic Harold Bloom, whose opinions have lost little credibility despite the fact that he was led astray by Donald Foster, displays his unabashed love for the bard in his eloquent ode to "Shakespeare's Universalism"—Bloom takes the question, "Why Shakespeare?" and answers it passionately and even persuasively during those stretches when he's not comparing Will to a god. On the other hand, we have George Bernard Shaw, a curmudgeon who made a virtual career out of disparaging Shakespeare. Shaw begs to differ in his alternately satiric and serious harangue against "Bardolatry"—"We must get rid of reputations," he writes, and he means particularly the reputation of Shakespeare who was, to his mind, a very poor moral philosopher and therefore highly overrated.

So is Shakespeare overrated? I don't care, let's party! The final section, "Fun & Games," provides a sampling of Shakespearean fun, from the intellectually stimulating to the downright silly to the pop cultural. We have crossword puzzles, quizzes to test your knowledge of everything you've learned so far, a madlib for your next *Hamlet*-themed mixer, and a list (because everyone loves lists) of "Shakespeare on Screen" (because you can only read so much).

The point of this final section and this whole Companion, for that matter, is something I'm sure you already know since you're holding this book right now—Shakespeare is fun! Really fun. Yeah, he's witty and wise, maybe someone else, possibly gay, a turner of a good phrase, a god among men to some readers and vastly overrated to others, but he's also fun. So have a blast reading this Shakespearean miscellany, and before you dive into the weird and wonderful world of William of Stratford-upon-Avon (or maybe some other place), enjoy this poem that probably wasn't written by him.

A Funeral Elegy

Since Time, and his predestinated end,
Abridg'd the circuit of his hopeful days,
Whiles both his Youth and Virtue did intend
The good endeavors of deserving praise,
What memorable monument can last
Whereon to build his never-blemish'd name
But his own worth, wherein his life was grac'd—
Sith as [that] ever he maintain'd the same?
Oblivion in the darkest day to come,
When sin shall tread on merit in the dust,
Cannot rase out the lamentable tomb
Of his short-liv'd deserts; but still they must,
Even in the hearts and memories of men,

Claim fit Respect, that they, in every limb
Rememb'ring what he was, with comfort then
May pattern out one truly good, by him.
For he was truly good, if honest care
Of harmless conversation may commend
A life free from such stains as follies are,
Ill recompensed only in his end.
Nor can the tongue of him who lov'd him least
(If there can be minority of love
To one superlative above the rest
Of many men in steady faith) reprove
His constant temper, in the equal weight
Of thankfulness and kindness: Truth doth leave
Sufficient proof, he was in every right
As kind to give, as thankful to receive.
The curious eye of a quick-brain'd survey
Could scantly find a mote amidst the sun
Of his too-short'ned days, or make a prey
Of any faulty errors he had done—
Not that he was above the spleenful sense
And spite of malice, but for that he had
Warrant enough in his own innocence
Against the sting of some in nature bad.
Yet who is he so absolutely blest
That lives encompass'd in a mortal frame,
Sometime in reputation not oppress'd
By some in nothing famous but defame?
Such in the By-path and the Ridgeway lurk
That leads to ruin, in a smooth pretense
Of what they do to be a special work
Of singleness, not tending to offense;
Whose very virtues are, not to detract
Whiles hope remains of gain (base fee of slaves),
Despising chiefly men in fortunes wrack'd—
But death to such gives unrememb'red graves.
 Now therein liv'd he happy, if to be
 Free from detraction happiness it be.
His younger years gave comfortable hope
To hope for comfort in his riper youth,
Which, harvest-like, did yield again the crop
Of Education, better'd in his truth.
Those noble twins of heaven-infused races,
Learning and Wit, refined in their kind
Did jointly both, in their peculiar graces,
Enrich the curious temple of his mind;
Indeed a temple, in whose precious white
Sat Reason by Religion oversway'd,
Teaching his other senses, with delight,
How Piety and Zeal should be obey'd—
Not fruitlessly in prodigal expense
Wasting his best of time, but so content
With Reason's golden Mean to make defense

Against the assault of youth's encouragement;
As not the tide of this surrounding age
(When now his father's death had freed his will)
Could make him subject to the drunken rage
Of such whose only glory is their ill.
He from the happy knowledge of the wise
Draws virtue to reprove secured fools
And shuns the glad sleights of ensnaring vice
To spend his spring of days in sacred schools.
Here gave he diet to the sick desires
That day by day assault the weaker man,
And with fit moderation still retires
From what doth batter virtue now and then.
But that I not intend in full discourse
To progress out his life, I could display
A good man in each part exact and force
The common voice to warrant what I say.
For if his fate and heaven had decreed
That full of days he might have liv'd to see
The grave in peace, the times that should succeed
Had been best-speaking witnesses with me;
Whose conversation so untouch'd did move
Respect most in itself, as who would scan
His honesty and worth, by them might prove
He was a kind, true, perfect gentleman—
Not in the outside of disgraceful folly,
Courting opinion with unfit disguise,
Affecting fashions, nor addicted wholly
To unbeseeming blushless vanities,
　　But suiting so his habit and desire
　　As that his Virtue was his best Attire.
Not in the waste of many idle words
Car'd he to be heard talk, nor in the float
Of fond conceit, such as this age affords,
By vain discourse upon himself to dote;
For his becoming silence gave such grace
To his judicious parts, as what he spake
Seem'd rather answers which the wise embrace
Than busy questions such as talkers make.
And though his qualities might well deserve
Just commendation, yet his furnish'd mind
Such harmony of goodness did preserve
As nature never built in better kind;
Knowing the best, and therefore not presuming
In knowing, but for that it was the best,
Ever within himself free choice resuming
Of true perfection, in a perfect breast;
So that his mind and body made an inn,
The one to lodge the other, both like fram'd
For fair conditions, guests that soonest win
Applause; in generality, well fam'd,
If trim behavior, gestures mild, discreet

Endeavors, modest speech, beseeming mirth,
True friendship, active grace, persuasion sweet,
Delightful love innated from his birth,
Acquaintance unfamiliar, carriage just,
Offenseless resolution, wish'd sobriety,
Clean-temper'd moderation, steady trust,
Unburthen'd conscience, unfeign'd piety;
If these, or all of these, knit fast in one
Can merit praise, then justly may we say,
Not any from this frailer stage is gone
Whose name is like to live a longer day—
Though not in eminent courts or places great
For popular concourse, yet in that soil
Where he enjoy'd his birth, life, death, and seat
Which now sits mourning his untimely spoil.
And as much glory is it to be good
For private persons, in their private home,
As those descended from illustrious blood
In public view of greatness, whence they come.
Though I, rewarded with some sadder taste
Of knowing shame, by feeling it have prov'd
My country's thankless misconstruction cast
Upon my name and credit, both unlov'd
By some whose fortunes, sunk into the wane
Of plenty and desert, have strove to win
Justice by wrong, and sifted to embane
My reputation with a witless sin;
Yet time, the father of unblushing truth,
May one day lay ope malice which hath cross'd it,
And right the hopes of my endangered youth,
Purchasing credit in the place I lost it.
Even in which place the subject of the verse
(Unhappy matter of a mourning style
Which now that subject's merits doth rehearse)
Had education and new being; while
By fair demeanor he had won repute
Amongst the all of all that lived there,
For that his actions did so wholly suit
With worthiness, still memorable here.
The many hours till the day of doom
Will not consume his life and hapless end,
For should he lie obscur'd without a tomb,
Time would to time his honesty commend;
Whiles parents to their children will make known,
And they to their posterity impart,
How such a man was sadly overthrown
By a hand guided by a cruel heart,
     Whereof as many as shall hear that sadness
     Will blame the one's hard fate, the other's madness;
Whiles such as do recount that tale of woe,
Told by remembrance of the wisest heads,
Will in the end conclude the matter so,

As they will all go weeping to their beds.
For when the world lies winter'd in the storms
Of fearful consummation, and lays down
Th' unsteady change of his fantastic forms,
Expecting ever to be overthrown;
When the proud height of much affected sin
Shall ripen to a head, and in that pride
End in the miseries it did begin
And fall amidst the glory of his tide;
Then in a book where every work is writ
Shall this man's actions be reveal'd, to show
The gainful fruit of well-employed wit,
Which paid to heaven the debt that it did owe.
Here shall be reckon'd up the constant faith,
Never untrue, where once he love profess'd;
Which is a miracle in men, one saith,
Long sought though rarely found, and he is best
    Who can make friendship, in those times of change,
    Admired more for being firm than strange.
When those weak houses of our brittle flesh
Shall ruin'd be by death, our grace and strength,
Youth, memory and shape that made us fresh
Cast down, and utterly decay'd at length;
When all shall turn to dust from whence we came
And we low-level'd in a narrow grave,
What can we leave behind us but a name,
Which, by a life well led, may honor have?
Such honor, O thou youth untimely lost,
Thou didst deserve and hast; for though thy soul
Hath took her flight to a diviner coast,
Yet here on earth thy fame lives ever whole,
In every heart seal'd up, in every tongue
Fit matter to discourse, no day prevented
That pities not thy sad and sudden wrong,
Of all alike beloved and lamented.
And I here to thy memorable worth,
In this last act of friendship, sacrifice
My love to thee, which I could not set forth
In any other habit of disguise.
Although I could not learn, whiles yet thou wert,
To speak the language of a servile breath,
My truth stole from my tongue into my heart,
Which shall not thence be sund'red, but in death.
And I confess my love was too remiss
That had not made thee know how much I priz'd thee,
But that mine error was, as yet it is,
To think love best in silence: for I siz'd thee
By what I would have been, not only ready
In telling I was thine, but being so,
By some effect to show it. He is steady
Who seems less than he is in open show.
Since then I still reserv'd to try the worst

Which hardest fate and time thus can lay on me.
T' enlarge my thoughts was hindered at first,
While thou hadst life; I took this task upon me,
To register with mine unhappy pen
Such duties as it owes to thy desert,
And set thee as a president to men,
And limn thee to the world but as thou wert—
Not hir'd, as heaven can witness in my soul,
By vain conceit, to please such ones as know it,
Nor servile to be lik'd, free from control,
Which, pain to many men, I do not owe it.
But here I trust I have discharged now
(Fair lovely branch too soon cut off) to thee,
My constant and irrefragable vow,
As, had it chanc'd, thou mightst have done to me—
But that no merit strong enough of mine
Had yielded store to thy well-abled quill
Whereby t'enroll my name, as this of thine,
How s'ere enriched by thy plenteous skill.
Here, then, I offer up to memory
The value of my talent, precious man,
Whereby if thou live to posterity,
Though't be not as I would, 'tis as I can:
     In minds from whence endeavor doth proceed,
     A ready will is taken for the deed.
Yet ere I take my longest last farewell
From thee, fair mark of sorrow, let me frame
Some ampler work of thank, wherein to tell
What more thou didst deserve than in thy name,
And free thee from the scandal of such senses
As in the rancor of unhappy spleen
Measure thy course of life, with false pretenses
Comparing by thy death what thou hast been.
     So in his mischiefs is the world accurs'd:
     It picks out matter to inform the worst.
The willful blindness that hoodwinks the eyes
Of men enwrapped in an earthy veil
Makes them most ignorantly exercise
And yield to humor when it doth assail,
Whereby the candle and the body's light
Darkens the inward eyesight of the mind,
Presuming still it sees, even in the night
Of that same ignorance which makes them blind.
Hence conster they with corrupt commentaries,
Proceeding from a nature as corrupt,
The text of malice, which so often varies
As 'tis by seeming reason underpropp'd.
O, whither tends the lamentable spite
Of this world's teenful apprehension,
Which understands all things amiss, whose light
Shines not amidst the dark of their dissension?
True 'tis, this man, whiles yet he was a man,

Sooth'd not the current of besotted fashion,
Nor could disgest, as some loose mimics can,
An empty sound of overweening passion,
So much to be made servant to the base
And sensual aptness of disunion'd vices,
To purchase commendation by disgrace,
Whereto the world and heat of sin entices.
But in a safer contemplation,
Secure in what he knew, he ever chose
The ready way to commendation,
By shunning all invitements strange, of those
Whose illness is, the necessary praise
Must wait upon their actions; only rare
In being rare in shame (which strives to raise
Their name by doing what they do not care),
As if the free commission of their ill
Were even as boundless as their prompt desires;
Only like lords, like subjects to their will,
Which their fond dotage ever more admires.
He was not so: but in a serious awe,
Ruling the little ordered commonwealth
Of his own self, with honor to the law
That gave peace to his bread, bread to his health;
Which ever he maintain'd in sweet content
And pleasurable rest, wherein he joy'd
A monarchy of comfort's government,
Never until his last to be destroy'd.
For in the Vineyard of heaven-favored learning
Where he was double-honor'd in degree,
His observation and discreet discerning
Had taught him in both fortunes to be free;
Whence now retir'd home, to a home indeed
The home of his condition and estate,
He well provided 'gainst the hand of need,
Whence young men sometime grow unfortunate;
His disposition, by the bonds of unity,
So fast'ned to his reason that it strove
With understanding's grave immunity
To purchase from all hearts a steady love;
Wherein not any one thing comprehends
Proportionable note of what he was,
Than that he was so constant to his friends
As he would no occasion overpass
Which might make known his unaffected care,
In all respects of trial, to unlock
His bosom and his store, which did declare
That Christ was his, and he was Friendship's Rock:
A Rock of Friendship figured in his name,
Fore-shewing what he was, and what should be,
Most true presage; and he discharg'd the same
In every act of perfect amity—
Though in the complemental phrase of words

He never was addicted to the vain
Of boast, such as the common breath affords;
He was in use most fast, in tongue most plain,
Nor amongst all those virtues that forever
Adorn'd his reputation will be found
One greater than his Faith, which did persever,
Where once it was protested, alway sound.
Hence sprung the deadly fuel that reviv'd
The rage which wrought his end, for had he been
Slacker in love, he had been longer liv'd
And not oppress'd by wrath's unhappy sin—
By wrath's unhappy sin, which unadvis'd
Gave death for free good will, and wounds for love.
Pity it was that blood had not been priz'd
At higher rate, and reason set above
Most unjust choler, which untimely Drew
Destruction on itself; and most unjust,
Robb'd virtue of a follower so true
As time can boast of, both for love and trust:
    So henceforth all (great glory to his blood)
    Shall be but seconds to him, being good.
    The wicked end their honor with their sin
    In death, which only then the good begin.
Lo, here a lesson by experience taught
For men whose pure simplicity hath drawn
Their trust to be betray'd by being caught
Within the snares of making truth a pawn;
Whiles it, not doubting whereinto it enters,
Without true proof and knowledge of a friend,
Sincere in singleness of heart, adventers
To give fit cause, ere love begin to end:
    His unfeign'd friendship where it least was sought,
    Him to a fatal timeless ruin brought;
Whereby the life that purity adorn'd
With real merit, by this sudden end
Is in the mouth of some in manner scorn'd,
Made questionable, for they do intend,
According to the tenor of the saw
Mistook, if not observ'd (writ long ago
When men were only led by Reason's law),
That "Such as is the end, the life proves so."
Thus he, who to the universal lapse
Gave sweet redemption, off'ring up his blood
To conquer death by death, and loose the traps
Of hell, even in the triumph that it stood:
He thus, for that his guiltless life was spilt
By death, which was made subject to the curse,
Might in like manner be reprov'd of guilt
In his pure life, for that his end was worse.
But O far be it, our unholy lips
Should so profane the deity above
As thereby to ordain revenging whips

Against the day of Judgment and of Love.
The hand that lends us honor in our days
May shorten when it please, and justly take
Our honor from us many sundry ways,
As best becomes that wisdom did us make.
The second brother, who was next begot
Of all that ever were begotten yet,
Was by a hand in vengeance rude and hot
Sent innocent to be in heaven set—
Whose fame the angels in melodious choirs
Still witness to the world. Then why should he,
Well-profited in excellent desires,
Be more rebuk'd, who had like destiny?
Those saints before the everlasting throne
Who sit with crowns of glory on their heads,
Wash'd white in blood, from earth hence have not gone
All to their joys in quiet on their beds,
But tasted of the sour-bitter scourge
Of torture and affliction ere they gained
Those blessings which their sufferance did urge,
Whereby the grace fore-promis'd they attained.
Let then the false suggestions of the froward,
Building large castles in the empty air,
By suppositions fond and thoughts untoward
(Issues of discontent and sick despair)
Rebound gross arguments upon their heart
That may disprove their malice, and confound
Uncivil loose opinions which insert
Their souls into the roll that doth unsound
Betraying policies, and show their brains,
Unto their shame, ridiculous; whose scope
Is envy, whose endeavors fruitless pains,
In nothing surely prosperous, but hope—
And that same hope, so lame, so unprevailing,
It buries self-conceit in weak opinion;
Which being cross'd, gives matter of bewailing
Their vain designs, on whom want hath dominion.
Such, and of such condition, may devise
Which way to wound with defamation's spirit
(Close-lurking whisper's hidden forgeries)
His taintless goodness, his desertful merit.
But whiles the minds of men can judge sincerely,
Upon assured knowledge, his repute
And estimation shall be rumor'd clearly
In equal worth—time shall to time renew 't.
The Grave—that in his ever-empty womb
Forever closes up the unrespected
Who, when they die, die all—shall not entomb
His pleading best perfections as neglected.
They to his notice in succeeding years
Shall speak for him when he shall lie below;
When nothing but his memory appears

Of what he was, then shall his virtues grow.
His being but a private man in rank
(And yet not rank'd beneath a gentleman)
Shall not abridge the commendable thank
Which wise posterity shall give him then;
For Nature, and his therein happy Fate.
Ordain'd that by his quality of mind
T' ennoble that best part, although his state
Were to a lower blessedness confin'd.
Blood, pomp, state, honor, glory and command,
Without fit ornaments of disposition,
Are in themselves but heathenish and [profaned],
And much more peaceful is a mean condition
Which, underneath the roof of safe content,
Feeds on the bread of rest, and takes delight
To look upon the labors it hath spent
For its own sustenance, both day and night;
Whiles others, plotting which way to be great,
How to augment their portion and ambition,
Do toil their giddy brains, and ever sweat
For popular applause and power's commission.
But one in honors, like a seeled dove
Whose inward eyes are dimm'd with dignity,
Does think most safety doth remain above,
And seeks to be secure by mounting high:
    Whence, when he falls, who did erewhile aspire,
    Falls deeper down, for that he climbed higher.
Now men who in a lower region live
Exempt from danger of authority
Have fittest times in Reason's rules to thrive,
Not vex'd with envy of priority,
    And those are much more noble in the mind
    Than many that have nobleness by kind.
Birth, blood, and ancestors, are none of ours,
Nor can we make a proper challenge to them,
But virtues and perfections in our powers
Proceed most truly from us, if we do them.
Respective titles or a gracious style,
With all what men in eminence possess,
Are, without ornaments to praise them, vile:
The beauty of the mind is nobleness.
And such as have that beauty, well deserve
Eternal characters, that after death
Remembrance of their worth we may preserve,
So that their glory die not with their breath.
Else what avails it in a goodly strife
Upon this face of earth here to contend,
The good t'exceed the wicked in their life,
Should both be like obscured in their end?
Until which end, there is none rightly can
Be termed happy, since the happiness
Depends upon the goodness of the man,

Which afterwards his praises will express.
Look hither then, you that enjoy the youth
Of your best days, and see how unexpected
Death can betray your jollity to ruth
When death you think is least to be respected!
The person of this model here set out
Had all that youth and happy days could give him,
Yet could not all-encompass him about
Against th'assault of death, who to relieve him
Strook home but to the frail and mortal parts
Of his humanity, but could not touch
His flourishing and fair long-liv'd deserts,
Above fate's reach, his singleness was such—
So that he dies but once, but doubly lives,
Once in his proper self, then in his name;
Predestinated Time, who all deprives,
Could never yet deprive him of the same.
And had the Genius which attended on him
Been possibilited to keep him safe
Against the rigor that hath overgone him,
He had been to the public use a staff,
Leading by his example in the path
Which guides to doing well, wherein so few
The proneness of this age to error hath
Informed rightly in the courses true.
As then the loss of one, whose inclination
Strove to win love in general, is sad,
So specially his friends, in soft compassion
Do feel the greatest loss they could have had.
Amongst them all, she who those nine of years
Liv'd fellow to his counsels and his bed
Hath the most share in loss: for I in hers
Feel what distemperature this chance hath bred.
The chaste embracements of conjugal love,
Who in a mutual harmony consent,
Are so impatient of a strange remove
As meager death itself seems to lament,
And weep upon those cheeks which nature fram'd
To be delightful orbs in whom the force
Of lively sweetness plays, so that asham'd
Death often pities his unkind divorce.
Such was the separation here constrain'd
(Well-worthy to be termed a rudeness rather),
For in his life his love was so unfeign'd
As he was both an husband and a father—
The one in firm affection and the other
In careful providence, which ever strove
With joint assistance to grace one another
With every helpful furtherance of love.
But since the sum of all that can be said
Can be but said that "He was good" (which wholly
Includes all excellence can be display'd

In praise of virtue and reproach of folly).
  His due deserts, this sentence on him gives,
  "He died in life, yet in his death he lives."
Now runs the method of this doleful song
In accents brief to thee, O thou deceas'd!
To whom those pains do only all belong
As witnesses I did not love thee least.
For could my worthless brain find out but how
To raise thee from the sepulcher of dust,
Undoubtedly thou shouldst have partage now
Of life with me, and heaven be counted just
If to a supplicating soul it would
Give life anew, by giving life again
Where life is miss'd; whereby discomfort should
Right his old griefs, and former joys retain
Which now with thee are leap'd into thy tomb
And buried in that hollow vault of woe,
Expecting yet a more severer doom
Than time's strict flinty hand will let 'em know.
And now if I have level'd mine account
And reckon'd up in a true measured score
Those perfect graces which were ever wont
To wait on thee alive, I ask no more
(But shall hereafter in a poor content
Immure those imputations I sustain,
Learning my days of youth so to prevent
As not to be cast down by them again)—
Only those hopes which fate denies to grant
In full possession to a captive heart
Who, if it were in plenty, still would want
Before it may enjoy his better part;
From which detain'd, and banish'd in th' exile
Of dim misfortune, has none other prop
Whereon to lean and rest itself the while
But the weak comfort of the hapless, Hope.
And Hope must in despite of fearful change
Play in the strongest closet of my breast,
Although perhaps I ignorantly range
And court opinion in my deep'st unrest.
But whether doth the stream of my mischance
Drive me beyond myself, fast friend, soon lost,
Long may thy worthiness thy name advance
Amongst the virtuous and deserving most,
  Who herein hast forever happy prov'd:
  In life thou liv'dst, in death thou died'st belov'd.

FINIS

The Man

"He was a man, take him all in all,
I shall not look upon his likes again."

—*Hamlet*, I,1,187

SHAKESPEARE AND HIS WORKS

by Margaret Miner and Hugh Rawson

William Shakespeare was born in 1564 in Stratford-upon-Avon, a market town in the English Midlands. His father, John, was a glovemaker, a dealer in agricultural produce, and a municipal official; his mother, Mary Arden, was the daughter of a well-to-do farmer. The first evidence of Shakespeare's existence is his baptism, recorded April 26 in the parish registry of Holy Trinity on the southern edge of town. The tradition that he was born three days before, on Sunday the 23rd, is appealing, because it would make his birthday coincide with St. George's Day, honoring England's patron saint. It also makes a fearful symmetry, for Shakespeare died on an April 23rd, fifty-two years later, in 1616.

In between, Shakespeare was a husband, father, actor, poet, and playwright. He married at eighteen a woman who was eight years older, Anne Hathaway. Their first child, Susanna, was born in 1583, followed by twins, Hamnet and Judith, in 1585. Hamnet died young, aged eleven, but the daughters lived to have families of their own. Their children had no children, however, so the last of Shakespeare's direct descendants was a granddaughter who died in 1670.

Shakespeare went to London in the 1580s. It is not known exactly when or why. He may have joined up with the Queen's Men, one of the five companies of traveling players that visited Stratford in 1587. Legend has it that he fled Stratford in order to avoid punishment for poaching. Once in London, he is said to have supported himself with odd jobs as a printer's devil and as a hired man for a livery stable, holding horses while his betters attended the theater. No real evidence exists for these stories.

By 1592, however, Shakespeare was well established not only as an actor but a playwright. This is certain, thanks to an attack published that year by a rival, Robert Greene, on "an upstart crow . . . that with his tiger's heart wrapped in a player's hide, supposes he is . . . the only Shake-scene in the country." And there are later references to Shakespeare as a "principal comedian" and a "principal tragedian." He is reported to have been particularly effective as the ghost in *Hamlet* and as Adam in *As You Like It*.

Shakespeare prospered. In 1594, he became a charter member of a theatrical company, the Lord Chamberlain's Men, later renamed the King's Men. In 1596, the Shakespeare family was granted a coat of arms. In 1597, William purchased the second-largest house in Stratford. In 1599, his acting company moved into the newly opened Globe Theater, in which Shakespeare had a one-tenth interest. (He is the only Elizabethan dramatist known to have received a share of a theater's profits.) In 1611, he retired.

Shakespeare made his will on March 25, 1616. He sought to keep his estate intact by leaving most of it to his daughter Susanna. His wife received, famously, the "second-best bed with the furniture." This may have been the bed they slept in, as opposed to the bed for guests, which was a better one, being less often used. Less than a month after making his will, Shakespeare was dead. On April 25, 1616, he was buried in the chancel of the church in which he had been baptized.

Aside from real estate and other worldly goods, Shakespeare left thirty-seven plays, 154 sonnets, and several longer poems. The exact numbers are in dispute. Shakespeare wrote only some parts of some of the plays, so different scholars come up with different totals. Some credit him with *Two Noble Kinsmen* (written with John Fletcher), which would increase the number of plays to thirty-eight. And suggestions continue to be made that he might have written other sonnets and poems of the period.

Even in cases where the authorship is certain, the dates of composition almost always depend on guesswork. The sonnets were published in 1609 but probably written at least a decade earlier. The dates of the other poems also are uncertain. For example, it was once thought that Shakespeare wrote *Venus and Adonis* before coming to London, but scholars now believe that it and *The Rape of Lucrece* were written in the period 1592-94, when playwrights had time on their hands because London's theaters were closed because of plague. As for the plays, their dates of composition generally must be deduced from entries in the register of the Company of Stationers; allusions to historical events; references in the works of other writers; mentions of them in diaries, account books, letters, and other records; and, of course, stylistic analysis. In most cases, there is plenty of room for argument.

Eighteen of the plays were published within Shakespeare's lifetime in small books called quartos. These vary a great deal in character, and quarto editions of the same play differ from one another in a number of instances. Some quartos have the plays in finished forms; other texts are very rough, perhaps based on actors' memories or shorthand notes rather than written scripts.

In 1623, seven years after Shakespeare's death, two actor friends, John Heminges and Henry Condell, collected thirty-six of his plays into what has come to be known as the First Folio. (*Pericles* is the only play in the official canon missing from this collection.) Some of the play texts in the First Folio are the same as those in previously published quarto editions. In other cases, new material seems to have been added or else cuts and condensations have been made. This complicates the dating problem, since it raises the possibility that some topical allusions may have been inserted while revising plays composed some years earlier.

With all these caveats, it remains possible to devise at least a rough chronology of Shakespeare's works. The following listing is taken from Sylvan Barnet's general preface to the Signet Classic Shakespeare Series.

Plays

1588-93	The Comedy of Errors
1588-94	Love's Labour's Lost
1590-91	2 Henry VI
1590-91	3 Henry VI
1591-92	1 Henry VI
1592-93	Richard III
1592-94	Titus Andronicus
1593-94	The Taming of the Shrew
1593-95	The Two Gentlemen of Verona
1594-96	Romeo and Juliet
1595	Richard II
1594-96	A Midsummer Night's Dream
1596-97	King John
1596-97	The Merchant of Venice
1597	1 Henry IV
1597-98	2 Henry IV
1598-1600	Much Ado About Nothing
1598-99	Henry V
1599-1600	Julius Caesar
1599-1600	As You Like It
1599-1600	Twelfth Night
1600-01	Hamlet
1597-1601	The Merry Wives of Windsor

1601-02	Troilus and Cressida
1602-04	All's Well That Ends Well
1603-04	Othello
1604-05	Measure for Measure
1605-06	King Lear
1605-06	Macbeth
1606-07	Antony and Cleopatra
1605-08	Timon of Athens
1607-09	Coriolanus
1608-09	Pericles
1609-10	Cymbeline
1610-11	The Winter's Tale
1611-12	The Tempest
1612-13	Henry VIII

Poems

1592	Venus and Adonis
1593-94	The Rape of Lucrece
1593-1600	Sonnets
1600-01	The Phoenix and the Turtle

THE AUTHORSHIP DEBATE
by Joseph Sobran

And this man is now become a god.

A fter four centuries, Shakespeare remains the most haunting of authors. He seems to know us better than we know him. He has put our deepest feelings into his own magnificent language, which, though now semiarchaic, still fills us with "wonder and astonishment," as Milton wrote. But he seems to escape all our attempts to know him: "[Shakespeare's] personality always evades us, even in the Sonnets," as Harold Bloom observes in *The Western Canon*. And for over a century now, the Shakespeare authorship question has appeared to be a strange circus at the edge of the town of literary studies. We are told not to waste too much time there, nor expect to find anything profound. Professional Shakespeare scholars question the good sense, the competence, and even the sanity of authorship heretics—the anti-Stratfordians, as they are usually called—and commonly charge them with a snobbish refusal to believe that a man of modest origins and education, who was born and died in a provincial town, could have been the greatest genius in English literature.

There is good reason for the scholars' dismissive attitude. Until I was nearly forty, I shared it myself. From my early teens through graduate school (I planned to make a career of Shakespeare studies), I never for a moment doubted the authorship of "the Stratford man," as the heretics call him—the phrase still makes me uneasy. And a great deal of the heretical literature is outlandish.

Still, I always found the standard Shakespeare biographies—those of Sidney Lee, Marchette Chute, Peter Quennell, F. E. Halliday, A. L. Rowse, and Samuel Schoenbaum—oddly frustrating. They never managed to connect. The author seemed unrelated to his work. How could this nondescript man have created Falstaff and Cleopatra? I assumed that if we knew more about him, we would have some sort of answer. We at least had his will, written shortly before his death in 1616. Why didn't that will contain a single bright turn of phrase? How could Shakespeare write even a thousand words without leaving his touch? I was puzzled, disappointed, but not yet skeptical. Like a good soldier, I suppressed my doubts, even after leaving graduate school for a career in journalism.

The difficult of knowing Shakespeare the man has been summed up with unusual candor by an orthodox scholar, Irvin Leigh Matus:

> It was said of William Shakespeare that "In the shadowy throng of the Great he cuts an uninspiring figure." He certainly is an elusive one. During his lifetime we do hear something of the poet and playwright in contemporary sources, but of the man himself little more than business transactions and lawsuits. One letter exists that was written to him, but not one written by him. Takes of Shakespeare abound, but they did not begin to surface until fifty years or more after his death—there is only one contemporary anecdote. Of the numerous documents in which his name appears there are five legible signatures of "William Shakespeare," but it is not certain all are by his hand. Even when his play *Richard II*, long associated with the ambitions of the Earl of Essex, became a prelude to rebellion, Shakespeare is not once mentioned in the trial that sent the Earl to the block. Thus, although his genius was acknowledged in his lifetime, Shakespeare himself stubbornly insists upon remaining in the shadows . . .

A few years ago, when I began to be persuaded that there was more to this story than the conventional view, I entered a bizarre world of colorful people, totally unlike the academic world I'd known before.

The anti-Stratfordian tradition had begun with the champions of Francis Bacon, who in their heyday a century ago specialized in finding cryptograms and anagrams claiming Bacon's authorship buried in the plays. The first renowned Baconian, coincidentally named Delia Bacon, is renowned for her attempt to dig up Shakespeare's bones in the hope of proving her namesake's title to the works. From there it only got wilder. The cipher craze began with a fiery American congressman and utopian reformer named Ignatius Donnelly, who in 1888 published a thousand-page tome called *The Great Cryptogram: Francis Bacon's Cipher in the So-Called Shakespeare Plays*. Donnelly also credited Bacon with the so-called works of Marlowe, Montaigne, and many others—780 plays in all. Others followed suit, in the apparent conviction that *Hamlet* and *King Lear* were less interesting as tragedies than as brainteasers. One erudite Baconian, Sir Edward Durning-Lawrence, discovered that the playfully pedantic word *honorificabilitudinitatibus* in *Love's Labour's Lost* could be rearranged to read *Hi ludi F. Baconis nati tuiti orbi*, or "These plays, F. Bacon's offspring, are preserved for the world." Rarely has classical learning been put to such ingenious use.

Other candidates eventually included Christopher Marlowe and various earls—of Oxford, Derby, Rutland, Essex, and Southampton. Among the more unlikely candidates who have been advanced are Elizabeth I, James I, Anne Hathaway, and Daniel Defoe. Setting aside whatever case may exist for their majesties or Mrs. Shakespeare, Defoe was not even born until 1629, after nearly all the Shakespeare works had been published!

During the 1940s, Percy Allen, a leading Oxfordian, converted to a theory of group authorship after conducting interviews at séances with the shades of Oxford, Bacon, and Shakespeare. He published his conversations with these three worthies, over the anguished pleas of what I suppose we must call mainstream Oxfordians, in a little book titled *Talks with Elizabethans.* The three collaborators did agree that chief credit for their plays belonged to Oxford. Bacon told Allen, "I wrote none of the plays; but I was fortunate in being consulted frequently. A circle of interested parties was formed; I had the honour of being one of those. I also acted as critic and adviser. You understand. It was a case of joint authorship." Shakespeare, for his part, allowed: "I am responsible for parts of the plays, and for suggestions as to production of the plays. . . . I was quick at knowing what would be effective on the stage. I would find a plot, consult with Oxford, form a skeleton edifice which he would furnish and people, as befitted the subject." Oxford confirmed this: "My work was but the filling of a frame, in most cases. I would have you know that I never wrote a play from the beginning to the end. I filled in the framework." (He recalled Shakespeare himself as "a good friend of mine" and "an entertaining rogue.") Orthodox scholars received these revelations with reserve, and cackles.

One leading Oxfordian, renowned for his temper, accused me of implying that he and other Oxfordians were either fools or liars because I had spelled the Stratford man's name "Shakespeare" rather than "Shakspere"—the prescribed form among anti-Stratfordians, who attach great significance to the matter—in a short article on the authorship question: Fallings-out among different anti-Stratfordian sects, or divisions within them, are common. A Baconian of my acquaintance was refused admittance to an Oxfordian Internet group because of his schismatic views—Baconians and dogs need not apply! Oxfordian factions, after complaining that their ideas are denied a fair hearing by orthodox scholars, often conspire to squelch dissident opinions at their own gatherings. The suggestion that Oxford was bisexual is enough to make some of his partisans livid: apparently, he must not only be accorded the glory of authorship but must also be, as far as possible, idealized.

At one point I was approached by a rich old lady who, having learned that I was a professional writer with an interest in the authorship question, arranged for me to visit her at her Mississippi home. This woman shared with me her somewhat fantastic beliefs about various amorous intrigues at the court of Elizabeth I; she had even written, and published at her own expense, a book on these matters in doggerel verse. I found her charming but almost incomprehensible. At length she offered me a staggering amount of money—she mentioned a million dollars—to write a book, in prose if necessary, arguing not only that Edward de Vere, seventeenth Earl of Oxford, was the true author of the Shakespeare plays, but that Oxford had secretly begotten the Earl of Southampton on Elizabeth herself (a notion widely held by Oxfordians, who consider this supposed liaison romantic rather than dishonorable). She specified a number of other pet ideas that the proposed book must include: for example, that Southampton had been the rightful king of England, bastard though he was. I tried hard to see it her way, but I just couldn't follow her reasoning. To my occasional regret, I turned her down.

On the other hand, the heretics have included people of intellectual, literary, and artistic distinction: Walt Whitman, Henry James, Mark Twain, John Galsworthy, Sigmund Freud, Vladimir Nabokov, David McCullough. Several are notables of theater and cinema: Charlie Chaplin, Orson Welles, Sir John Gielgud, Michael York, and Kenneth Branagh. Yet these famous anti-Stratfordians have made no important contributions to the debate. Only Twain, in his pamphlet *Is Shakespeare Dead?*, wrote about the authorship question at any length. The bulk of the anti-Stratfordian literature has been produced by a few amateur scholars and a great many eccentrics.

In fact, the great comedy of the authorship question is that so many important discoveries have been made by dubious scholars, intellectual misfits, and outright cranks; mainstream scholars, meanwhile, ignoring their challengers, have insisted that there is no real authorship question at all. Under the circumstances, we do well to set aside credentials (which can carry their own whiff of snobbery) and sift all the evidence carefully. I have learned how often a priceless gem may be found in a pile of intellectual rubbish. More than once I have been reminded of St. Paul's dictum that God has chosen the foolish things of this world to confound the wise.

Samuel Schoenbaum, foremost among recent orthodox biographers, derides "the dark power of the anti-Stratfordian obsession." But we should not leap to the conclusion that the heretics have eaten of the insane root that takes the reason prisoner; many, in fact, appear quite normal. As a cruel fate would have it, one of the shrewdest of them was named Looney (rhymes, I hasten to add, with "bony")—John Thomas Looney, who first named the Earl of Oxford as the real author. Twain (more or less Baconian), Sir George Greenwood (agnostic), Calvin Hoffman (Marlovian), and Charlton Ogburn

Jr. (Oxfordian) exemplify the best of the anti-Stratfordian advocates. Suffice it to say that thousands of sane readers have found all of them to some extent compelling, and that any cause has to be judged by the case made by its ablest advocates.

The orthodox scholars' methods are cautious enough to make their conclusion plausible. And though I sympathize with the heretics in their challenge to the received view, their methods are often so haphazard as to make them sound hysterical. Skeptical of "the Stratford man," they can be astoundingly credulous about their pet candidates. Their faults are not the ravings of lunacy, but the almost unavoidable errors of isolation from a stabilizing mainstream. Professional scholars constantly criticize each other and harmonize their findings; amateurs, living in a more anarchic state, rely too much on self-criticism. The Shakespeare heretics have produced an abundance of wild fruits, but so far these have never been carefully sorted. The authorship question needs an overhaul.

The deeper trouble with most of the anti-Stratfordian theories, aside from illogicalities and deficiencies of evidence, is that they have very little *literary* relevance. They have nothing to do with our experience of reading Shakespeare or watching the plays in performance; they reduce the interest of a supreme poet to the level of a whodunit with a creaky plot. Shakespeare becomes a gigantic puzzle, to which the solution is "F. Baconis." Even if a theory of that kind were true, it would tell us nothing about the Shakespeare works except that the wrong name had been attached to them—leaving us to wonder why the prosaic rationalist Bacon would write a haunting sonnet like "No longer mourn for me when I am dead." Bacon must have written the great plays and poems only for the purpose of proving that Shakespeare didn't.

The excesses and fantasies of some heretics do not endear them to the professional scholars, and they make any alternative authorship theory seem hopelessly farfetched. The scholars believe, with every appearance of common sense, that Shakespeare was born in Stratford-upon-Avon, received a good education at the local school, married young, had three children, went to London, became a successful actor and playwright, wrote a few nondramatic poems along the way, bought property in Stratford, finally retired there, and died in 1616.

Yet this "official" account of Shakespeare's life also fails to offer any literary insights. Its apparently sensible premise never brings us close to the mind and heart of the author himself. Indeed, unbeknownst to many, the orthodox account teems with difficulties and has never successfully answered certain basic questions.

For example: How did Shakespeare know so much about court life, heraldry, law, Ovid, and Italy, as the plays suggest? The orthodox answer is that he did not. The scholars all agree that he got a sound education in his hometown, supplemented that knowledge sufficiently for his purposes through his own reading, and still made gaffes no highly educated man would have made—giving Bohemia a seacoast, for example, and making his characters travel by water between the inland cities of Verona and Milan. The standard view is that Shakespeare acquired much of his wide knowledge casually, perhaps from the thousands of travelers, merchants, soldiers, and sailors who milled about in Elizabethan London and frequented its taverns. Gareth and Barbara Lloyd Evans offer a hypothetical anecdote: "The dusty traveller sitting in the Mermaid Tavern in London, just arrived from wars on the Continent, never realized what was to happen to his replies when the quiet stranger sipping his beer turned and asked him—'How is it with you, cos?'" The legendary Mermaid Tavern becomes Mermaid University, with Shakespeare its most distinguished alumnus. It seems a reasonable supposition—at least not impossible.

The late Louis B. Wright, in the introduction to the Folger Library series of Shakespeare plays, disposes of the authorship question in one patronizing remark:

> The anti-Shakespeareans base their arguments upon a few simple premises, all of them false. These false premises are that Shakespeare was an unlettered yokel without any schooling, that nothing is known about Shakespeare, and that only a noble lord or the equivalent in background could have written the plays. The facts are that more is known about Shakespeare than about most dramatists of his day, that he had a very good education, acquired in the Stratford Grammar School, that the plays show no evidence of profound learning, and that the knowledge of kings and courts evident in the plays is no greater than any intelligent young man could have picked up at second hand. Most anti-Shakespeareans are naive and betray an obvious snobbery. The author of their favorite plays, they imply, must have had a college diploma framed and hung on his study wall like the one in their dentist's office, and obviously so great a writer must have had a title or some equally significant evidence of exalted social background. They forget that genius has a way of cropping up in unexpected places and that none of the great creative writers of the world got his inspiration in a college or university course.

Schoenbaum writes sardonically of the growth of authorship heresy: "In the fullness of time, alternative candidates were offered, preferably candidates with university degrees and blue blood coursing through their veins." After recounting the story of Delia Bacon, one of the first to champion the cause of her namesake Francis Bacon as Shakespeare, he adds:

Other dissidents have since championed Bacon, or argued for one earl or another: Oxford, or Derby, or Rutland—almost any earl will do. These anti-Stratfordian theories do not agitate the great majority of readers or playgoers, or those professionally concerned with Shakespeare and his times. As children of a democracy, we do not need to be persuaded of the potentialities for literary accomplishment in plebeian citizens—even the offspring of unlettered immigrants.

Other academic biographers agree. Gerald Eades Bentley accuses the heretics of "irresponsible fancy" and remarks "the great majority [of them] share the firm conviction that the author must have been a blue-blooded aristocrat." Russell Fraser charges the heretics with "snobbery": they believe that the real author must be endowed with "either noble lineage or academic honors." Stanley Wells indicts them for both "snobbery" and "the desire for self-publicity."

These chiding remarks show how deeply democratic ideology has become entwined with the cultural icon known as "William Shakespeare." The issue is not merely factual; it is moral, political, and even spiritual. For twentieth-century readers, Shakespeare without his plebeian identity wouldn't quite be Shakespeare. In his recent book *The Western Canon*, Harold Bloom celebrates Shakespeare in strikingly extraliterary terms: "There is an inverse ratio, a little beyond our analytical skills, between Shakespeare's virtual colorlessness and his preternatural dramatic powers. . . . The creator of Hamlet and Lear died a not very momentous death after an uneventful life. There are no great biographies of Shakespeare, not because we do not know enough but because there is not enough to know. . . . At once no one and everyone, Shakespeare *is* the Western Canon." Shakespeare the man is "ordinary-seeming" and "unassuming," even "someone with whom you could have a relaxed drink," in Bloom's view. That is precisely what makes his genius so astounding. The less flamboyant his outward show, the more miraculous his genius appears. Two other recent commentators, Germaine Greer and Garry O'Connor, agree in calling Shakespeare "invisible."

But to suspect that the real Shakespeare was a lord, or at least a courtier, may not necessarily be snobbery; it may be sociology. The ardent democrat Walt Whitman sensed the hand of one of the "wolfish earls" in Shakespeare's comedies, which he pronounced "non-acceptable to democracy." As Whitman shows, one needn't be a partisan of the feudal nobility to raise the authorship question. The real issue is not whether anti-Stratfordian views reveal the reactionary sympathies of the doubter, but whether the Shakespeare plays suggest an author of privileged background—one who not only received the best education available, but who also knew court life, traveled widely, and enjoyed other advantages beyond the reach of a man of rustic origins, however intelligent. In the end, calling the Shakespeare plays works of genius tells us very little about them. "Genius" is not an explanation. Nor is it a motive. We can't make up the deficit in our knowledge of Shakespeare with superlatives. *A Streetcar Named Desire* may not be as great a play as *Hamlet,* but the author of *Hamlet* couldn't have written it and Tennessee Williams could. This is a matter not of genius but of individuality.

The fact is that we know very little about Shakespeare—certainly not enough to warrant 300- to 600-page "biographies" that inflate a few dry documents, mostly business records, into the semblance of a full life. Most readers would be surprised to learn that the actual records of the first half of Shakespeare's life consist of five spare entries in parish registers: the date of his baptism, the date of his betrothal, the date and terms of his marriage, the dates of his three children's baptisms (two of whom were twins). Everything else from those years—1564 to 1590—must be deduced.

Furthermore, there is no match between the known facts about the man and the works assigned to his authorship. Shakespeare's life and personality have no discernible relation to the plays and poems bearing his name. As Emerson put it, "I cannot marry the life to the work." It is not only that we lack information. We don't know much about most of his contemporaries either, but nobody doubts that Marlowe, Spenser, and Jonson wrote the works ascribed to them. Even from the meager records and rumors that we have, Marlowe sounds like just the sort of man who would write Marlowe's works. The same may be said of Spenser and Jonson. Consider other great European poets. "Of Dante's life we know as little as we know of Shakespeare's," Pablo Milano writes. "Yet the harmony between Dante's character and his work is such that the meager facts are almost enough for us." The same could be said of Virgil. We do know a lot about Milton, and his identity has never been in question. But doubts about Shakespeare have actually increased as time has passed.

The name "Shakespeare" itself may be germane. The family name was usually spelled "Shakspere" in Stratford. This may or may not signify something important; Elizabethan spelling is notoriously irregular and it is hard to be sure. I would leave the matter there, but anti-Stratfordians of all denominations tend to treat it as definitive evidence that the man of Stratford wasn't "Shakespeare" the author; the debate over this point has been endless and inconclusive.

The distinction between "Shakspere" and "Shakespeare" does, however, have one convenience for this book. For clarity's sake, I will call the Stratford gentleman "Mr. Shakspere" and the author in dispute "Shakespeare." Whether they are the same man is, of course, the question.

By 1623, two dozen works, some of them spurious, had been published bearing the name William Shakespeare but not identifying the author further. It was in 1623 that the First Folio of the plays appeared, identifying Shakespeare with Mr. Shakspere of Stratford. If this testimony had not pegged Mr. Shakspere as the author, and the works had come down to us with no name attached, it would probably never have occurred to anyone to suggest that he had written them. Nothing in the records or impressions of his life would lead us to believe he was a writer at all, or anything but an actor and shareholder in a London theater company and a successful businessman in his hometown.

The Folio has given us the famous woodcut portrait of Shakespeare by Martin Droeshout—though this dull, pudgy face has been supplemented, in modern iconography, with a more seemly countenance, based on the Chandos portrait: lean, high-domed, goateed, with penetrating eyes and an earring. The experts admit that the authenticity of the Chandos portrait is doubtful, but it has certainly provided us with an arresting image of Shakespeare: intellectual but rather swashbuckling, rather like a psychoanalyst with a dash of pirate in him.

Unfortunately, the Folio is sparing with the kind of information we crave about Shakespeare. It omits such essential facts as the dates of his birth and death; it offers no anecdotes or reminiscences by friends. It praises him lavishly without actually describing him. It doesn't include the two narrative poems, *Venus and Adonis* and *The Rape of Lucrece*, for which he was most famous in his own time, or his self-revealing Sonnets or minor poems. The Folio tells us that Mr. Shakspere wrote the plays between its covers, nothing more. The scholars, taking his authorship largely on faith, have been forced to piece his life together as best they can from other sources. Later generations have emulated the Folio in lauding Shakespeare's universality— "his infinite variety"—at the expense of any *individuality.*

Whoever he was, he was not, in Professor Bloom's phrase, "at once no one and everyone"—or a man who never had to blot a line, as the Folio suggests. The superlatives used to describe Shakespeare tell us nothing useful about Mr. Shakspere.

As a result, dozens of questions about Mr. Shakspere have never been fully answered by the scholars, despite their best efforts. For instance: How did he zoom from being a young man in the provinces, with a wife and three children as of 1585, to being the most polished poet in England, writing amorous verses to a young nobleman, by the early 1590s? Nothing is known of this crucial period, known to scholars as "the lost years." Yet almost as little is known of Mr. Shakspere's years in London, when he should have been at the height of his success and fame. His death in 1616 apparently passed unnoticed in the city that adored the plays and poems bearing his name. And as we shall see, some of the most impenetrable mysteries have been posed by the one work that would seem to tell us most about the poet himself: the little book published in 1609 as *Shake-peares Sonnets*.

Some may still ask: What difference does it make who Shakespeare really was, as long as we have the plays? It is a perfectly sensible question. The Elizabethans felt the same way. They weren't curious about authors. Being interested in poetry rather than in the poet's psyche, they no more considered a play a self-revelation of the playwright than they considered a table a self-revelation of the carpenter. Drama, a popular art, was public and self-explanatory. Nobody sought hidden depths in it. For better or worse, we moderns are different. We *are* curious. We have made literary biography a genre. We can't always justify it theoretically, and we debate endlessly about the relation between art and the artist, but we want a peek at him anyway.

When it comes to the Sonnets, the poems don't make much sense unless we know something about the sonneteer himself. Most of the scholars try to shoo us away from taking a biographical interest in these intimate poems, even though the Sonnets, unlike the plays, are explicitly about real people—at least four of them, including the poet. That poet sounds so unlike Mr. Shakspere that the scholars are driven to classify the Sonnets as fictions, in spite of all evidence to the contrary.

It has become fashionable in recent literary criticism, notably in the extreme school of deconstruction, to deny the relevance of the author—an awkward postulate for would-be biographers. It is odd to find the biographers saying much the same thing. Whatever justification our personal interest in Shakespeare may have, I can only say that I feel no need to apologize for it. Our curiosity is too natural and too common to be blushed at. Like millions of others, I am interested in who Shakespeare was as a simple matter of historical fact; and if the doctors of literature condemn our inquiry, we can appeal to the historians.

Further, if we are accused of snobbery for doubting Mr. Shakspere's authorship, we can reply that a sort of inverted snobbery seems to be driving his partisans. And it does seem strange that an author whose biases are so obviously aristocratic should be made an icon and test of democratic faith. Whoever Shakespeare was, he seems to have taken little interest in the sort of self-made man his champions suppose him to have been.

Finally, we must face the charge of crankery, or even lunacy, for pursuing this inquiry at all. This charge has been given its fullest expression by Schoenbaum:

In certain recurring features of anti-Stratfordian behavior we may discern a pattern of psychopathology. The heretic's revulsion against the provincial and lowly; his exaltation of his hero (and, through identification, himself) by furnishing him with an aristocratic, even royal, pedigree; his paranoid structures of thought, embracing the classic paraphernalia of persecution: secrets, curses, conspiracies; the compulsion to dig in churches, castles, river beds, and tombs; the auto-hypnosis, spirit visitations, and other hallucinatory phenomena; the descent, in a few cases, into actual madness—all these manifestations of the uneasy psyche suggest that the movement calls not so much for the expertise of the literary historian as for the insight of the psychiatrist. Dr. Freud beckons us.

Taken to its limit, this approach implies that rational discussion of Shakespeare's authorship is pointless, since anyone who rejects the orthodox view must be somewhat crankish; it also implies that cranks can be persuasive only to other cranks. If so, orthodox scholars who try to stop the susceptible from being seduced are wasting their breath, while there is no need to warn normal people against the anti-Stratfordians, since normality itself is sufficient to immunize them.

One can understand Schoenbaum's psychoanalytic conceit as a joke, or even as a burst of exasperation with the generally prolix, often fanciful, and sometimes occult anti-Stratfordian literature, in which 800-page tomes are the norm. A sober scholar who has read them all may be pardoned for a bit of spleen. Still, he shows little compassion for the putatively diseased wits of the heretics; he evidently judges them more to be censured than pitied.

Schoenbaum's is a common attitude among the orthodox scholars, who seem a shade too eager to stigmatize the doubters and to warn others away from them. They assume that there is no fate worse than being an isolated crank, and that the threat of being excommunicated by academia should suffice to keep others in line.

The most dispiriting trait of the professional scholars is not their consensus about Shakespeare's identity, but *their refusal to admit that there can be any room for doubt.* Realizing very well how little is known about Mr. Shakspere of Stratford, they should at least allow for an agnostic middle ground. It is one thing to say that the testimony in favor of Mr. Shakspere's authorship remains, on balance, more satisfying than all the arguments made against it. It's quite another matter to concede nothing to dissent, or even uncertainty. In the writings of orthodox scholars on the anti-Stratfordian heresies, it is rare to find a concessive note. Animadversions, often vituperative, are the rule. It is almost never admitted that any of the heretics has ever raised a point worth taking into account. The impulse to scold the dissenter; the inability to acknowledge even the possibility of reasonable doubt; suspicion even of the noncommittal; the denial of ambiguities in our imperfect records of the past; intense frustration with anything less than unanimity; the conviction that dissent reveals a moral or psychological defect—these are the marks of the brittle belief systems we call cults or ideologies, as opposed to the balanced judgment that tries to come to terms with all the available evidence.

WHAT DID SHAKESPEARE READ?
by Leonard Barkan

Warwickshire illiterate; supplier of story-lines to the groundlings; Renaissance polymath. You show me your Shakespeare, and I'll show you a hypothesis about the size and character of his library. We have no hard facts about Shakespeare the reader: no personal documents, no inventories, no annotated volumes with his bookplate. And though his dramatic characters often turn up with books in their hands (sometimes merely *pretending* to read them), we have no neatly autobiographical equivalent of the opening moment in Sir Philip Sidney's *Astrophil and Stella*, where the struggling poet consults pages from his predecessors' work. The impossibility of answering the question only adds to its allure, promising to tell us both who Shakespeare was and how he wrote. Do we see the collected works as the product of an uncanny alchemy of sophistication and complexity performed by a provincial with moderate education and limited book-learning? Are they the output of an extraordinarily hard-working craftsman who had a knack for taking what was mostly second-rate contemporary writing and transforming its superficial excitements into more profound forms of high sensation? Or should we accept the proposition that the plays and poems represent a full engagement in the high culture of early modern Europe? In these responses to the matter of Shakespeare's reading one can trace both the history of his reputation and the changing fashions of his critics.

Of all these possibilities, Shakespeare the unlettered country boy deserves most immediate attention because it is the place where both biography and criticism begin. The famous lines on the subject, from the poem that introduces the First Folio, possesses every kind of precedence and authority:

> Soul of the age!
> The applause, delight, the wonder of our stage!
> My Shakespeare, rise: I will not lodge thee by

Chaucer or Spenser, or bid Beaumont lie
A little further, to make thee a room;
Thou art a monument without a tomb,
And art alive still while thy book doth live,
And we have wits to read, and praise to give . . .
For if I thought my judgement were of years,
I should commit thee surely with thy peers:
And tell how far thou didst our Lyly outshine,
Or sporting Kyd, or Marlowe's mighty line.
And though thou hadst small Latin, and less Greek[1] . . .

Ben Jonson, as ever greatest of collaborators and most problematic of friends, is so masterful an epigrammatist that this last concessive clause will inspire centuries of lore concerning what Shakespeare read. His motives are complex, to say the least, and the very fact that the phrase gets wrenched out of context will only serve to intensify the mixed messages. Jonson is writing a traditional poem of praise and not, at least on the face of it, giving Shakespeare a grade in classics. Rather he begins with a simple paradox, appropriate to issuing the "Complete Works" seven years after their author's demise: the man is dead, the works live on. In the lines quoted above, Shakespeare is awarded his enduring place within the English Dead Poets' Society; then the subject shifts to his competition with the ancients. The proposition—and it must trouble Jonson, of all people—is that an English writer might enter the company of immortals whom he does not know how to read.

Not that Jonson is being altogether ingenuous. He is himself by auto-proclamation the most learned of authors who descended into the popular world of the theatre. And the classical form of his praise reminds us that there are other writers with large Latin and more Greek. But ancient languages and literatures may not be the ultimate issue here. Jonson's project is to make us understand that Shakespeare is a poet of nature first and of art second; and even if one strand of humanism from the Renaissance to Alexander Pope will declare that Homer and nature are the same, we inevitably inherit a Shakespeare who achieved his magic while being a mediocre reader of the ancients.

Whether that estimate is true or not, there is, alternatively, a large part of Shakespeare's library which Jonson would never have advertised in his eulogy, that enormous body of writings which has been collected under the rubric "Sources of Shakespeare's Plays." While some of the material is itself Latin and Greek, this part of Shakespeare's reading has tended to be quite segregated from the canon that Jonson had in mind. However well or badly we imagine Shakespeare knew them, the authors implied in the Folio poem are learned humanist forebears who shed lustre on any modern writer operating under their influence; and that influence itself is understood as operating via a complex set of intellectual mediations. Shakespeare's "sources," on the other hand, are likelier to be minor figures, sometimes contemporary, often appearing in a sort of *Reader's Digest* form of publication; and this influence, far from being construed as subtle or cerebral, expresses itself as instrumental, opportunistic, or even plagiarizing. The two kinds of reading generally refer to different moments in Shakespeare's life, i.e., his schooling in Stratford vs. his daily work as the provider of some two scripts a year to a busy London theatrical company. They have also experienced quite separate fortunes in criticism. The classical predecessors, as we have seen, are launched in the very earliest texts promulgating Shakespeare, while in later times they contribute to philosophical and theoretical approaches to the plays. The sources begin to be of interest only in the eighteenth century, when they are often treated as signs of Shakespeare's lack of originality; subsequently, they fuelled whole industries of pedantic attempts to nail down a precise point of origin for his every text.

Our purpose here will be to consider all of this as one related body of material, to declare that "what Shakespeare read" consists of a lifetime of experience with text, both that which he found in preexisting books and that which he composed. In opening up the space between the reading and the writing, our topic turns out to be the most old-fashioned and the most new-fashioned of critical subject matters, resting upon all of the scholastic analyses of Shakespeare's grammar school or his sources, while it raises those modern epistemological doubts that have clustered around source, influence, individual authorship, and the ownership of language.

We have no personal information about Shakespeare's education and therefore no direct sense of the texts he studied as a child. It is, however, reasonable to assume that he attended the King's New School in Stratford-upon-Avon; and, since there is abundant documentation concerning many primary and grammar schools throughout England at that time, it is not difficult to reconstruct both a list of texts and a sense of educational techniques. Pupils began with their ABC's and early on worked to master English by reading religious texts like simple catechisms and the Psalms. As early as the age of six or seven, "grammar school" would begin, which, of course, meant Latin grammar.

He we can postulate a plausible book-list for the Stratford boy. William Lily's Latin Grammar, first compiled near the beginning of the sixteenth century and still in use two hundred and fifty years later, was the universal foundation. The first part, written in English and known as the *Shorte*

Introduction (or, more colloquially, the *Accidence*), took the student through the rudiments of grammar and inflection. In the second part, called the *Brevissima Institutio*, instruction was itself in Latin, covering morphology, syntax, figures of speech, and prosody. During these same early grades pupils were being put through texts of simple maxims in readily construable Latin. The *Sententiae pueriles* of Leonhardus Culmannus, which first appeared in the 1540s, consisted of a graded sequence of truisms, beginning with two words, then progressing to three, and so on. Of even wider usage was the *Disticha moralia* ascribed to Cato; here, too, the emphasis is on enduring verities appropriate to schoolboys, including exhortations to assiduousness, sexual morality, heroism, and acceptance of death. Similar again, both for its aphoristic quality and for its anthology form, was the notably influential Latin version of Aesop's *Fables*, also read in the first years of instruction.

The next phase of Latin readings included another classical-style compendium, the *Zodiacus Vitae* of Palingenio (written c. 1528, also popular in its English tranlsation by Barnabe Goge, first published in the 1560s), a twelve-book poetic farrago full of proverbial lore but including some substantial materials from antique culture relating to astronomy, metaphysics, and natural philosophy. Also at this time the schoolboy Shakespeare would have been presented with the first instances of what we would recognize as literature. Not that they are necessarily the most auspicious names. The first, Terence, formed one of the bases for Latin instruction all over Europe because his dialogue was thought to give the fullest impression of the way classical Latin was actually spoken; but lest we picture the infant proto-playwright mapping out his career as he construes the *Eunuch*, it should be pointed out that there is small trace of Terence in Shakespeare and far more of Plautus, who was decidedly less popular in the schools. The other threshold literary figure was Battista Spagnuoli (1447-1513), author of a set of eclogues entitled the *Bucolica*. The vast popularity of Mantuan, as he was always called, remains a historical mystery: whatever the reason, for the later Renaissance he was the supreme master of the bucolic mode, heir to his countryman Virgil (and sometimes thought to be superior to him), the official first teacher of poetics and cradle of pastoralism.

All this was generally mastered by the age of twelve: small Latin indeed. In the Upper School, the reading list covered most of the canonical Latin corpus. Some of these authors, like Ovid, will count for more in Shakespeare's works than they did in the curricula; others, like Virgil, less. For the most part, however, the allusiveness of Shakespeare's language (and of the culture in which he lived) is so universal that it is difficult to superimpose school reading upon playwriting with precision. Poets such as Horace, Juvenal, and Persius certainly stuck in the dramatist's mind, though they hardly seem to be foundational; the same could be said of the leading prose writers in the curriculum, such as Sallust and Caesar. Indeed, Shakespeare's relation to the high literary canon in Latin seems so personal, so different from a replication of assigned reading, that we might suppose him a dropout somewhere in his early teen years.

But that would be a mistake, given a quite different subset of schoolboy classical readings. To us the above great names represent the inevitable summit of ancient Latinity. But in an early modern education such as Shakespeare's, the progression is not from language to literature but from grammar to rhetoric. Thus the real focus of reading in the middle and upper school years—and here Shakespeare's studious familiarity is beyond dispute—is on that body of texts devoted to oratory. The foundation work is the *Ad Herennium,* then attributed to Cicero, which offered a complete structural account of diction, speech, argument, and style. In combination with the *Topics* of Cicero (an authentic work) and, for the upper forms, the *Institutio oratoriae* of Quintilian, this body of school texts not only introduced pupils to the advanced study of language but also formed the basis for all the study of logic that found its origins in Aristotle and its dissemination in every facet of intellectual and public life. Any account of law or medicine, of political theory or natural history, of ethics or metaphysics— indeed, literary criticism itself, so far as it exists in this period—can be traced to systems of thought and expression that are inculcated by this reading list in advanced rhetoric.

I use the term "reading list" precisely in its limiting sense. From beginning grammar to the classicizing language of all the professions, we should note *how* as well as *what* the student was reading. Pupils were learning another language almost from the time they began school, but the two languages were construed in fundamentally different ways. It is almost as true in Shakespeare's time as in Dante's that grammar is a property of Latin and not of the vernacular. It follows that the study of classical language is *structural*; in other words, we hear only about mastering grammar and syntax and never about mastering vocabulary. Both the early presence of an alternative language and the bias toward a systemic linguistics produce a consciousness of language as a thing in itself and not just as a frictionless instrument. But the mechanics of the learning process leave even more tangible marks. From the very beginnings of instruction, the method appears to have been question and answer: that is, language as a school subject is performed as a dramatic conversation. Once the basic patterns have been explored through these verbal exchanges, text itself takes the form of *sententia*. The first Latin readings in the curriculum, as we have seen, are collections of maxims; further, students were led through them in such a manner that the achievement of correct Latin was signaled by their finding of the appropriate verbatim *sententia,* like "amor vincit omnia" or "comparatio omnis odiosa est," thus identifying correct language and abiding truth as one and the same package.

None of this centres on the practice of translation. That activity—rather curiously, given modern method—is focused upon the rendering of English into Latin rather than the reverse. The texts most commonly chosen are themselves revealing: collections of English *sententiae,* whose correct rendering presumably recapitulates their classical origins; or, certain books from the (already translated) Bible, especially Psalms, Proverbs, or the apocryphal Ecclesiasticus, which, once again, can be readily rendered in the form of pithy sayings. Thus pupils are creating their own new Latin out of familiar English. As time goes on, however, they are doing something more. The summit of translation activity in the schoolroom, propounded by Roger Ascham and based on Cicero, required the pupil to go back and forth from a Latin text to an English translation to a reinvented Latin and so on until perfect competence was achieved. This remarkable exercise enforces complex relations between replication and originality: students keep inventing as they travel across the language barrier until they achieve a text that is at once their own voice and the re-creation of a preexisting model. What begins as a make-work exercise involving elementary school Latin will culminate in a more complicated relation to the major canonical writers of classical prose and poetry.

If translation was the capstone for grammar, then original composition formed the principal activity for the more advanced training in rhetoric. The first steps in this direction were oral, even dramatic: pupils and master held question-and-answer conversations in Latin. But soon reading and writing are closely intertwined. At the most basic level, they strung together *sententiae* into "themes," thus moving out from the proverbial lore of their reading into slightly more expanded sententiousness. With the more advanced readings, like the *Ad Herennium* or Ovid's *Heroides,* they began to compose epistles in prose or verse; finally they were expected to produce full-blow orations. All these educational processes consist of creative composition emerging from a set of readings that are at once theoretical and exemplary, offering both precept and prototype. Here the work depended on post-classical workbooks emerging out of Cicero and Quintilian, including the *Epitome* of Susenbrotus and the *Progymnasmata* of Aphthonius. More than their loftier predecessors, these texts were used interactively: they directed pupils essentially to place themselves in hypothetical or imaginative situations, sometimes historical, sometimes mythological, and to create their own Latin text. The resulting exercises were inevitably full of tropes, self-conscious about their status as discourse, and—most important of all—they amounted to dramatic impersonations. So, to descend to a perhaps simplistic historical comparison, while we have for decades taught college students to express their own selves and are rewarded with a fundamentally solipsistic public discourse, Renaissance education taught its upper grammar school students to impersonate other voices, and they were rewarded with a flowering of public oratory and theatre.

Finally, there is one other major author—the only modern—whose influence shaped the process of an English sixteenth-century education. In a series of texts on education, including the *Institution hominis Christiani*, the *De ratione studii*, and the *Institutio principis Christiani*, and in a set of close personal relations with John Colet, Dean of St. Paul's, Erasmus had laid out nearly all the principles of modern education. It is Erasmus who gives official status to the logical line that goes back towards Cicero and Aristotle and forward towards Descartes—that is, a set of stable and coordinated relations between truth and language. It is Erasmus who establishes the canon of classical authors suitable for instruction, and it is he who enforces the heuristic and moral value of the *sententia* in reading matter (it was his edition of Cato that was widely used in school), while also relegating purely sententious, often spuriously classical, works to a secondary position in favour of a moralistic literary criticism applied to major writers. It is Erasmus who shows the way to students, both in his *De conscribendis epistolis* and in his *Colloquies*, in the first demonstrating how to place letter-writing in a dramatic context and in the second offering the fullest modern example of humanistic discussion in multiple voices written in fine classical Latin. Then, at the highpoint of grammar-school education, came his famous *De Copia*, which offered both precept and example in the composition of language that was elegant, highly figured, and capable of almost infinite variation. Whether Shakespeare read Erasmus or not, he certainly had an Erasmian education.

The marks of all these processes and influences are written everywhere in Shakespeare's text. A simple census of all the Latin that appears in the playtexts reveals how many of the phrases are traditional maxims, traceable to early education. Often they are taken specifically from Lily's Latin Grammar, as for instance Sir Andrew's "Not to be abed after midnight is to be up betimes, and *diliculo surgere* [to rise at dawn], thou knowest" (*Twelfth Night*, II,3,1-2) or Tranio's "If love have touched you, naught remains but so— / *Redime te captum quam queas minimo* [Ransom yourself from captivity at the lowest possible price]" (*Shrew*, I,1,155-56), which is actually misquoted just as it is in Lily's Latin Grammar; indeed, when Horace's oft-repeated "Integer vitae [The man upright in life]" is cited in *Titus Andronicus* (IV,2,20), Chiron actually says, "I read it in the grammar long ago." Whether vernacular or classical, Shakespeare's usage is deeply imbued with *sententiae*; and some of the most famous of his riffs on traditional expressions, like "All the world's a stage" or "We are such stuff as dreams are made on," derive from Latin tags learned in school. Even Shakespeare's Bible shows evidence of his classical training: the books he most commonly cites are just the same Psalms, Proverbs, and Ecclesiasticus that he translated into Latin as a schoolboy.

On a number of occasions Shakespeare actually stages primary education. In *The Taming of the Shrew*, Lucentio, impersonating a Latin tutor to gain access to Bianca, follows the schoolroom practice of construing, or translating. His text is from the first book of Ovid's *Heroides*; but, given his amorous purposes, the translation he offers is, to say the least, idiosyncratic: "'*Hic ibat*,' as I told you before—'*Simois*,' I am Lucentio—'*hic est*,' son unto Vincentio of Pisa—'*Sigeia tellus*,' disguised thus to get your love . . ." (III,1,31-3). Bianca, *herself* no mean pupil, returns the translation exercise, as students were expected to do: "'*Hic ibat Simois*,' I know you not—'*hic est Sigeia tellus*,' I trust you not . . ." (III,1,40-1). (Her translation at least has the virtue of keeping the Latin clauses logically together. For the record, the lines actually mean, "Here flowed the Simois, here lies the Sigeian land.") *The Merry Wives of Windsor* includes a whole scene explicitly taken from instruction in Lily's Grammar, referred to as the "accidence." Here the construing is misconstrued not only by deliberate deception, but by the ignorance of the (female) onlookers, who turn innocent Latin into off-colour English, and by the mediocre performance of the pupil, William, in response to his Welsh schoolmaster, Evans. He does reasonably well with the basics, such as *hic*, *hæc*, *hoc*, but he comes aground in the more advanced translation practice:

> *Evans.* What is "lapis," William?
> *William.* A stone.
> *Evans.* And what is a "stone," William?
> *William.* A pebble.
> *Evans.* No, it is "*lapis*." I pray you remember in your
> prain.
> *William.* "*Lapis*."

William fails at the Cicer-Ascham translation method, i.e., Latin to English and back to Latin.

Love's Labour's Lost is above all Shakespeare's monument to the problems of grammar and rhetoric; there is hardly a scene that does not contain exercises in semantics or translation or else larger theories of language. Critical to the whole enterprise is the trio of (pseudo-) learned characters: Don Armado, the new-style wit; Nathaniel, the half-educated priest; and, of special interest here, Holofernes the classically trained schoolmaster. More pedant than pedagogue, Holofernes speaks in a perpetual construing from Latin to English; he cites numerous schoolbook *sententiae*; he quotes and comments on Mantuan as well as Ovid; he lords it over his fellow-"scholars"; he offers time-honoured and conservative views on English orthography.

Just how deeply these forms of reading and learning penetrated Shakespeare's invention may be observed most fully in a scene where no actual schoolmaster appears. It is an exchange between Touchstone and William in *As You Like It*:

> *Touchstone.* . . . Is thy name William?
> *William.* William, sir.
> *Touchstone.* A fair name. Wast born i' th'forest here?
> *William.* Ay, sir, I thank God.
> *Touchstone.* Thank God—a good answer . . . You do love this maid?
> *William.* I do, sir.
> *Touchstone.* Give me your hand. Art thou learned?
> *William.* No, sir.
> *Touchstone.* Then learn this of me: to have is to have. For it is a figure in rhetoric that drink, being poured out of a cup into a glass, by filling the one doth empty the other. For all you writers do consent that *ipse* is he. Now you are not *ipse*, for I am he.
> *William.* Which he, sir?
> *Touchstone.* He, sir, that must marry this woman. Therefore, you clown, abandon—which is in the vulgar, leave—the society—which in the boorish is company—of this female—which in the common is woman; which together is, abandon the society of this female, or, clown, thou perishest; or, to thy better understanding, diest; or, to wit, I kill thee, make thee away, translate thy life into death, thy liberty into bondage. I will deal in poison with thee, or in bastinado, or in steel. I will bandy with thee in faction, I will o'errun thee with policy; I will kill thee a hundred and fifty ways.
> (V,1,19-52)

The learned fool treats his hapless interlocutor to an almost complete performance of the grammar-school education that an Arden rustic cannot have experienced for real. First, catechism; then, the central proposition of dialectic, which lies at the heart of the relations among grammar, rhetoric, and logic, transmitted in terms of "ipse" and "cups" via Cicero and Quintilian,[2] then, the practice of construing from one language to another, in this case, from Lofty to Bumpkin; finally, as a graduation exercise, an invention in the spirit of Erasmus' *De copia*, except that where the original merely offered multiple ways of *saying* something (specifically, "Thank you for your letter"), Touchstone's diverse formulations provide multiple ways of *doing* something, i.e., murdering William by elegant variation.

Whether the grammar-school curriculum surfaces in the voice of the pedant or the parodist, it tells us something. For one thing, these textual materials nearly always betray an awareness that people speak many languages: Evans's instruction in *The Merry Wives of Windsor* is confusing less because of the Latin than because he is rendering both languages via Welsh; Touchstone affects to accommodate the language of the country; and the would-be lovers in *The Taming of the Shrew* are attempting to invent private languages. Further, all these appearances of early curricula delineate a world that is inescapably alternative to that of real (i.e., theatrical, or lived) experience. The texts of grammar, rhetoric, and literature, when rendered *as* texts, are in a profound sense bracketed—as are, of course, the characters who import them. Brilliant or foolish, these individuals speak of that which is external, unlived, or, at best, exemplary rather than real; and even when the characters are not marginal, like Hamlet when he appears to be citing Juvenal ("the satirical slave says here that old men have grey beards . . .") (II,2,196-7), their reading forms part of a textual alternative to actual experience.

Still, if the real issue is how such reading might be assimilated, it is best to understand Holofernes and Touchstone as polar opposites. The schoolmaster, it must be remembered, has great ambitions as a poet, producing, first, a laboured alliterative epigram on the hunting of the deer and then the (blessedly) fragmented pageant of the Worthies. Like his own creator, in other words, he travels the distance between old reading and new writing. Just how catastrophic this travel may be is demonstrated by his own literary criticism of one of the play's competing poets, the sonneteering Biron:

> for the elegancy, facility, and golden cadence of poesy—*caret* [i.e., is lacking]. Ovidius Naso was the man. And why, indeed "Naso" but for smelling out the odoriferous flowers of fancy, the jerks of invention. *Imitari* is nothing. So doth the hound his master, the ape his keeper, the tired horse his rider. (IV,2,114-18)

The irony is, of course, that Holofernes imagines himself to be on the side of invention over imitation when his poetry is agonizingly, almost regurgitatingly, derivative from the books that he inculcates and the pedantic languages that he speaks. The further irony is that true invention can emerge only from a properly understood practice of imitation. Young William Page may move pointlessly from *lapis* to *stone* and back to *lapis*. But that same system of instruction also allows for the alien, bracketed, frequently ancient, and always garbled prior text to become one's own voice, indeed, to define what that voice is. Such an achievement—the pun must be forgiven, since it is Shakespeare's—is the touchstone of the real poet.

A man is sitting in London around 1600 in the middle of a personal library whose catalogue corresponds precisely to the "Sources of Shakespeare's Plays": what can we say about his reading taste? Voracious; more middlebrow than highbrow; heterodox; philosophically not of the avant-garde; anglo-centric in certain ways, generally having to do with past and present public institutions, yet at the same time revealing a considerable fondness for continental storytelling. He is something of a history buff—in that field, his holdings range from the learned to the ephemeral. Theatre, represented a bit sparsely by comparison, is both classic and contemporary, with a sprinkling of university closet drama. There is a certain taste for current events, especially at the level of political intrigue and lifestyles of the rich and famous: these are often to be found in the pamphlet collection. As for highbrow literature, you are more likely to find a few well-thumbed volumes that a complete catalogue of the major works.

But let us name the names. As for the serious favourites, Ovid and Plutarch are visible everywhere, and Seneca is only a little less prominent. For classical history, apart from Plutarch, Livy was most often studied, but it is noteworthy that the real source may have been the *Epitome* of Livy written by Florus in the second century A.D. Other historians seem to have been consulted only for specific projects: Scotland, Denmark, and Turkey (this last for *Othello*) occasioned specialized research, while *Julius Caesar* appears to have required a lot of supplementary reading, including Tacitus, Appian, and perhaps Sallust and Suetonius.

Among Shakespeare's sources in his own language, the largest share belongs to the chroniclers who furnished material for the history plays. The compendia that he read most exhaustively were Edward Hall's *Union of the Two Noble and Illustre Famelies of Lancastre and Yorke* (1548), the *Chronicles* of Raphael Holinshed (1578, 1587), and John Stow's *Chronicles of England* (1580) and *Annales of England* (1592). Together, these offered the dramatist not only the raw data, both dynastic and anecdotal, but also the methodologies of history-writing and the special politics of the Tudor ascendancy. Of a different kind, but persistently influential, are such literary works as the didactic *Mirror for Magistrates* (1559) and Samuel Daniel's poetic *First Fowre Bookes of the Civile Wars* (1595), while yet another approach to the materials comes from the strenuous polemics for the Protestant cause offered by John Foxe in his *Acts and Monuments,* known as the *Booke of Martyrs* (first published in English, 1563). Figures of exceptional cultural fascination, including King John, Richard III, Henry V, and Falstaff had generated their own specialized source materials.

On what we would consider the more literary side, Shakespeare's English-language reading list tended to be similar to ours. So far as the fourteenth-century masters are concerned, Chaucer is writ large in *A Midsummer Night's Dream* and *Troilus and Cressida,* while John Gower makes his mark both at the very beginning of the dramatist's career (*Comedy of Errors*) and the very end (*Pericles*). The two greatest nondramatic masterpieces of Shakespeare's own age, Sir Philip Sidney's *Arcadia* and Edmund Spenser's *Faerie Queene,* find their way into comic, historic, and tragic works, with *King Lear* embracing elements of both.

Shakespeare's tastes were not exclusively highbrow, however. Among the works of prose fiction, Barnaby Riche's *Apolonius and Silla* (1581), Robert Greene's *Pandosto* (1588), and Thomas Lodge's *Rosalynde* (1590) might be forgotten today were they not the principal sources for *Twelfth Night, The Winter's Tale,* and *As You Like It,* but they prove to be lively works in their own right that vindicate Shakespeare's dependence on them. John Lyly's *Euphues* (1579), whose mix of wit and eros and pedantry swept through Elizabethan literate culture, can be detected in the language of every overwrought lover in the comedies. So far as theatrical literature is concerned, Shakespeare's tastes are decidedly popular. While Marlowe and Jonson exercise some influence, it appears that Anon. is virtually his favourite dramatist, as witness his careful reading of *The Troublesome Reign of King John* (1591), or the complex ways in which *The Rare Triumphes of Love and Fortune* (1589) and *Mucedorus* (first version, 1598) are woven into the plots of the late romances.

Lists of titles like these need to be grounded in a larger sense of the contemporary intellectual climate, particularly as regards book-making and book-reading. At the level of European culture in general, two factors must not be forgotten: first, the continental Renaissance, now more than a century old, had stimulated an enormous opening-up in the category of literature, both that which was revived from the past and that which was being newly produced; second, the invention and growth of printing continued to disseminate the material objects of reading in greater quantity and to a wider audience. England, besides feeling these effects, was by the later sixteenth century in the grip of a quite self-conscious drive to found and promote a national—or even nationalist—literary culture, the evidence of which is not only such highly visible careers as those of, say, Spenser and Ralegh, but also a flood of literary rivalries and disputes which generated a great deal of ink and rendered book-making itself a matter of public interest. Indeed, these sometimes became the actual stuff of drama, as is clear from the frequent appearance of names like Gabriel Harvey, Thomas Nashe, Robert Greene, and George Chapman in the explanatory notes to Elizabethan playtexts.

Two other matters bear even more directly on Shakespeare's sources as a body of text. From the 1560s onwards, a gigantic industry of translation revolutionizes what it is possible for the English to read. Though the dramatist's familiarity with passages in the original is often demonstrable, Shakespeare's would scarcely have been possible without: Hoby's Castiglione (1561), Adlington's Apuleius (1566), Golding's Ovid (1567), North's Plutarch (1579), Harington's Ariosto (1591), Chapman's Homer (1598, in part), Holland's Livy (1600), Fairfax's Tasso (1600), and Florio's Montaigne (1603). To say that is, of course, to return to "small Latin and less Greek": as a reader, Shakespeare was pretty much like most of us who have a reasonable command of a foreign language. Faced with the bulk of something like the *Orlando Furioso*, we would still prefer a reliable trot; and the chances of our experiencing the whole work and of going back to it in the original are vastly increased by the existence of a good translation. The translations cited above are, for the most part, better than good: they are brilliantly imaginative, if not always accurate by our standards, and some of them, particularly those in prose, helped create a new literary English. As Shakespearian reading, these works function in a variety of ways, ranging from idol perusal, to direct use as source, to material for minute verbal plagiarism. All the while they were putting him in touch with contemporary and past masterpieces, as well as with the phenomenon of multiple languages in the same space.

The other book-making circumstance, while related to the matter of translation, is much harder to pin down. The hypothetical Shakespearian source-library is notably rich in a kind of volume whose origins go back to the Middle Ages but whose international career is very much alive and well in the sixteenth century, namely, the compendium of stories. At the canonical peak of the genre is Boccaccio's *Decameron* (itself a Shakespearian source, relevant to *All's Well*, *Cymbeline*, and *Merry Wives*); other such texts include the *Gesta Romanorum*, which dates back to the thirteenth century, *Il Novellino* by Masuccio of Salerno (1476), the *Novelle* of Bandello (1554), *Il Pecorone* of Giovanni Fiorentino (1558), and *Gli Hecatommithi* of Giraldi Cinthio (1565), plus related versions in other languages including *Histoires tragiques* by Pierre Boaistuau (1559) and by François de Belleforest (1564), Geoffrey Fenton's *Certaine Tragicall Discourses* (1567), and William Painter's *Palace of Pleasure* (1567). Collectively, this body of material touches upon a remarkable range of Shakespearian texts—not only, as one might expect, tales of fantasy and love such as *Merchant, Pericles,* and *Cymbeline* but also those set in very different universes like *Merry Wives, Titus Andronicus, Timon of Athens,* and even *Hamlet.*

These collections of narratives in part represent an early modern codification (in some cases fabrication) of folktales; in their vast overlapping interrelations we can witness a whole field—call it literary bumper cars— where stories are made and remade via translation, imitation, elaboration, parody, and recombination. If, for instance, one follows the source trail of *Romeo and Juliet* or *Othello,* where there is a proximate originary work (Arthur Brooke's *Tragicall Historye of Romeus and Juliet* and Cinthio's *Hecatommithi*) but behind it a tangle of versions coming out of Bandello and his inheritors, one is struck by the difficulty of pinning down Shakespeare's specific route of derivation, especially given questions concerning his familiarity with languages. But more than that, one notices that this range of material made available to the dramatist a kind of postgraduate course in comparative structural narratology. And even if these anthologies appear to be "literature lite," they also remind us that some of Shakespeare's most prestigious source books, including the *Metamorphoses* and Plutarch's *Lives,* are themselves structured in the form of composite and detachable parts that invite comparison.

Now, having listed all these points of origin, ancient and modern, lofty and popular, we must ask the slightly ingenuous question, did Shakespeare really *read* his sources? As I have suggested earlier, it is clear enough that he read his schooltexts quite independently of instrumentalizing them for some new piece of writing. It is also clear that there is a body of important works of such universal presence within early modern civilization—one might borrow Foucault's designation of "transdiscursive," by which he refers to Marx and Freud—that they are present everywhere in the formation of the plays via some deep acculturation. One can hardly imagine, for instance, the erotic ideals of the Sonnets without Plato, or the politics of Milan and Naples in *The Tempest* without Machiavelli, or the transports of love, whether straight or parodied, from *Love's Labour's Lost* to *Antony and Cleopatra,* without Petrarch. Likewise, without the Bible we could not begin to account for turns of phrase like Hamlet's "There's a special providence in the fall of a sparrow" (V,2,157-8), or Bottom's "The eye of man hath not heard, the ear of man hath not seen . . ." (*Dream* IV,1,204-5), or, indeed, the very title *Measure for Measure,* with its multiple reverberations from the Sermon on the Mount. All of these books, in whatever form and by whatever necessary intermediaries—he *read.*

But centuries of source study, applying itself to Bandello, or the anonymous playtexts, or even the canonical classics which form the basis of the dramatic plots, have suggested that Shakespeare did not so much read these works as cut and paste them—that is, he opportunistically stole what he needed, ignored the rest, and sublimed everything. These assumptions are well worth questioning. To put the matter in its simplest terms, authors generally can discover something in another book only once they have read that book independently of its precise future usefulness. Shakespeare, in other words, might have consulted Richard Knolle's *Generall Historie of the Turkes* when he had already worked out the circumstances of *Othello*, but he is less likely to have dreamed up a tale about a Moor marrying a Venetian lady and then gone to a first reading of Cinthio's *Hecatommithi*, III,7, either accidentally or in the foreknowledge that he would find what he needed there. And by whatever chronology of consultation, exported material remains touched with its own original context. The source book, whether it is *The Faerie Queene* or *The Three Ladies of London,* enters a complicated calculus of inspiration for any author under its influence.

These abstract principles become concrete when we follow some quite specific paths of Shakespearian sourcing. In a set of interesting articles, Martin Mueller has shown how certain stories, while providing the main point of origin for a single play, also haunt the dramatist's imagination repeatedly and throughout his career. Bandello's tale of Fenicia and Timbreo includes all the main events of the Claudio and Hero plot in *Much Ado*, but elements in this story continue to generate important moments in later plays, including *Othello, Cymbeline,* and *The Winter's Tale*, where Shakespeare seems to be trying to do different things—generally less rational and more magical—with the Bandello source. Plutarch's *Life of Brutus* is a primary source for *Julius Caesar*, but the relation between Brutus and his wife Portia weaves itself through a set of variations on the conduct of married life in *The Merchant of Venice, I Henry IV*, and *Macbeth* (as well as *Lucrece*). In an equally persistent way, *The True Chronicle Historie of King Leir*, before it reaches its fullest expression, has already helped shape the way Shakespeare represents the state of nature in *As You Like It,* assassination in *Richard III* and *Hamlet*, and the competition among suitors in *The Merchant of Venice*.

Some of the associations Mueller draws may be tenuous, but he makes a strong case that most of Shakespeare's favourite sources were known to him by the time he was in his twenties. (Interestingly, the notable exceptions are narratives drawn from current events, like the case of Cordell Annesley, which provided materials for *Lear*, and the writings about Virginia voyages that formed a basis for *The Tempest*.) In Mueller's words, "It should therefore be a fundamental axiom of source criticism to observe the consequences of the fact that Shakespeare's readings jostled each other in his memory and settled in a complex web of memory pathways long before they became sources for plays he intended to write."[3] In effect, source study becomes not the map for a unidirectional pathway but a means to trace the reciprocal relation between distinctive features in Shakespeare's creative imagination and a library of texts which are themselves subject to revisionary reading and adaptation in light of that imagination.

If, for instance, we imagine a cluster of narrative elements including nobly born wives who are entangled for good or ill with their husbands' public lives (e.g., Lucrece, two Portias, Lady Percy, Desdemona, Lady Macbeth, Hermione), calumniated women presumed dead but merely sleeping (e.g., Hero, Hermione, Innogen, and—stretching the point a little—Desdemona), and fathers and daughters (too numerous to list), not only do we refer to the plots of half the plays but we also map out a very broad field of source relation that goes back to a relatively small number of originary texts. To literalize the process: Shakespeare finds the stories that replicate his personal obsessions; the stories give those obsessions certain shapes; he in turn reshapes them by producing every-varying adaptations; in the end he becomes a reader of, and source for, himself.

When Polonius asks Hamlet what he is reading, the Prince replies, "Words, words, words" (II,2,192). It's a joke from Hamlet's antic disposition, and a good one, since both Renaissance and modern psychology can readily picture madmen as losing the thread of sequential discourse and focusing instead on syntactically disconnected verbal units. For the purposes of literary criticism, however, such madness may be prerequisite. To identify Shakespeare's reading only by the larger structures derived from a classical education or the plots derived from preexisting narratives is to neglect the independent power of the word. This is not the place to rehearse all the by now familiar arguments from structuralism and post-structuralism concerning the "death of the author." Suffice it to say that both the structures of language and, more to the point, all the ambient vocabularies at a given historical or cultural moment contribute to the composition of any piece of writing as much as do the consciously manipulated materials traditionally classed as intellectual underpinnings or sources.

This kind of reading, for which Roland Barthes's felicitous term is the *déjà lu*, concerns us not just out of universal theoretical correctness but because Shakespeare proves to have been a kind of language sponge, a picker-up of specialized lexicons from every conceivable stratum of his society. In this field it would be impossible to give a full account of Shakespeare's library, or indeed of all the sequences of imagery and allusion in the plays that testify to his skills at absorption. Perhaps the clearest index to this phenomenon is the response of scholars who have attempted to account for this verbal adeptness by imagining a Shakespeare who was not so much a linguistic polymath as a real practising multiprofessional. Shakespeare has been, over the centuries, a lawyer, a doctor, a thief, a theologian, a Catholic, a Protestant, a duellist, a military man, a falconer, a keeper of hounds—all because he had mastered their respective languages.

Let us permit one quite respectable instance to stand for this kind of argument in general. A. F. Falconer argues that the opening scene of *The Tempest* is in every detail nautically correct. Expressions like "take in the topsail" and "lay her a-hold" do not represent mere colourful sea-talk but the perfectly phrased set of orders designed to save the ship under the given conditions of wind, shore, and ocean. From which Falconer concludes that Shakespeare "could not have come by this knowledge from books."[4] That may be true: there is no surviving sixteenth-century text in which all of these locutions are neatly laid out, and it is possible that the man who lived his whole life many days' arduous travel from the sea had managed to do some apprentice work aboard a sailing vessel, preferably among tars who had colourful tales to tell of the Bermuda triangle. But it is more likely—and the same would go for many other firsthand vocabularies—that Shakespeare derived this knowledge from a combination of reading, listening, and loving the play of language.

Perhaps it is Shakespeare's own fascination with books—or some attempt to exorcise that fascination—that turns so many of his characters into readers. Most of the time when book-learning enters the dramatic scene, as the example of *Love's Labour's Lost* has already suggested, it is in opposition to real experience. Love in particular seems to keep little company with reading. Some amorous bookmen are hopeless: Slender reveals his ineptitude as a lover by regretting that he has not brought Tottel's *Miscellany* to help him woo Anne Page (*Merry Wives* I,1,165); nor do we entertain higher hopes for Malvolio's prospects with Olivia when he determines to "read politic authors" (*Twelfth Night* II,5,141). But when Juliet tells Romeo that he kisses by the book (I,5,107), or when Rosalind-Ganymede reports on an uncle who read out lectures against love (*As You Like It* III,2,312), or when Lysander reports the lesson of all those tales and histories that "The course of true love never did run smooth" (*Dream* I,1,134), the place of reading appears more complicated. It is not so much a contradiction of experience as a necessary first step along the way.

And that dynamic points finally to Shakespeare's two greatest dramatic scenes of reading, one from the beginning of his career, the other from the end. The raped, mutilated, and silenced Lavinia of *Titus Andronicus*, in an attempt to reveal the horrors of her own experience, can do nothing but point to a book in which the story of Tereus, Procne, and Philomela has prewritten the miserable sequence of events. The precision of the parallel—although Shakespeare's version is more horrific—enables both the characters and the audience to read experience as though it were a book and read the book as though it were experience. Prospero's book, which he prizes above his dukedom, is both the sign and the substance of his magical power. When, at the end of the play, he drowns it "deeper than did ever plummet sound" (*Tempest* V,1,56), he and all those who have survived the shipwreck are returned to Europe, to politics, to life, death, and marriage—in short, to the fullness of natural experience. Lavinia's volume is quite explicitly Ovid's *Metamorphoses*, and while Prospero's is less directly identifiable, it is signalled by an incantation that comes almost verbatim from the same work. When Shakespeare's characters have their fullest experience of reading, they turn to Shakespeare's favourite source.

Notes

[1] Citation is to *Ben Jonson*, ed. Ian Donaldson (Oxford University Press, 1985), p. 454.

[2] See T. W. Baldwin, *William Shakspere's Small Latine and Lesse Greeke* (Urbana: University of Illinois Press, 1944), II, 116-20.

[3] Martin Mueller, "From Leir to Lear," *Philological Quarterly* 73 (1994), 197.

[4] A. F. Falconer, *Shakespeare and the Sea* (New York: F. Ungar, 1964), p. 39.

Reading List

Baldwin, T. W., *William Shakspere's Petty School* (Urbana: University of Illinois Press, 1943).

Baldwin, T. W., *William Shakspere's Small Latine and Lesse Greeke* (Urbana: University of Illinois Press, 1944).

Barkan, Leonard, *The Gods Made Flesh: Metamorphosis and the Pursuit of Paganism* (New Haven: Yale University Press, 1986).

Barthes, Roland, "The Death of the Author," in *Image Music Text,* trans. S. Heath (New York: Hill and Wang, 1977).

Bullough, Geoffrey, ed., *Narrative and Dramatic Sources of Shakespeare,* 8 vols. (London: Routledge and Kegan Paul, 1957-75).

Donaldson, E. Talbot, *The Swan at the Well: Shakespeare Reading Chaucer* (New Haven: Yale University Press, 1985).

Foucault, Michel, "What Is an Author?" in *Language, Counter-Memory, Practice,* trans. D. F. Bouchard and S. Simon (Ithaca, N.Y.: Cornell University Press, 1977).

Halpern, Richard, *The Poetics of Primitive Accumulation: English Renaissance Culture and the Genealogy of Capital* (Ithaca, N.Y.: Cornell University Press, 1991).

Jardine, Lisa, and Anthony Grafton, *From Humanism to the Humanities: The Institutionalizing of the Liberal Arts in Fifteenth- and Sixteenth-Century Europe* (London: Duckworth, 1986).

Lennox, Charlotte Ramsay, *Shakspear Illustrated: or, the Novels and Histories, on Which the Plays of Shakespear Are Founded* (New York: AMS Press, 1973 [first published in 1753-54]).

Lynch, Stephen J., *Shakespearean Intertextuality: Studies in Selected Sources and Plays* (Westport, Conn.: Greenwood Press, 1998).

Mueller, Martin, "From Leir to Lear," *Philological Quarterly* 73 (1994), 195-217.

Mueller, Martin, "*Hamlet* and the World of Ancient Tragedy," *Arion* 5 (1997), 22-45.

Mueller, Martin, "Plutarch's 'Life of Brutus' and the Play of Its Repetitions in Shakespearean Drama," *Renaissance Drama*, n.s. 22 (1991), 47-93.

Muir, Kenneth, *The Sources of Shakespeare's Plays* (New Haven: Yale University Press, 1978).

Orme, Nicholas, *Education and Society in Medieval and Renaissance England* (London: Hambledon Press, 1989).

Patterson, Annabel, *Reading Holinshed's Chronicles* (University of Chicago Press, 1994).

Salingar, Leo, *Shakespeare and the Traditions of Comedy* (London: Cambridge University Press, 1974).

Whitaker, Virgil K., *Shakespeare's Use of Learning: An Inquiry into the Growth of His Mind and Art* (San Marino, Calif.: Huntington Library, 1953).

WAS SHAKESPEARE GAY?

by Norrie Epstein

If Shakespeare were to apply for an NEA grant on the basis of the Sonnets, he would probably be denied one. There is profound resistance to accepting Shakespeare, the icon of Western civilization, as gay. High school teachers introduce Shakespeare's Sonnets as passionate love lyrics, neglecting to mention that they were written to a man, while many scholars read the poems as expressions of male friendship, ignoring their frank homoeroticism. But there's no getting around it: the Sonnets are clearly addressed to a young man, and even allowing for what professors call the "Renaissance cult of male friendship," many of the poems are quite ardent. It could be that editors have overemphasized the importance of this cult as a way of explaining away what would otherwise be undeniably homoerotic. Nonetheless, no other straight poet has ever written such ardent poems to another man. This doesn't mean that the poems can be understood or appreciated only as homosexual poems; they are universal lyrics about love—which happen to be addressed to a man. We'll never know whether the eroticism went beyond poetic imaginings or if the relationship was ever consummated. There has, however, been a conspiracy of silence concerning Shakespeare's sexuality.

In the ambiguous Sonnet 20, the poet suggests his sexual attraction to the young man, the "master-mistress of my passion," but he ends the sonnet by wittily pointing out that Nature has thwarted his amorous intentions:

> And for a woman wert thou first created,
> Till Nature as she wrought thee fell a-doting,
> And by addition me of thee defeated,
> By adding one thing to my purpose nothing.
> > But since she pricked thee out for women's pleasure,
> > Mine be thy love, and thy love's use their treasure.

("Thing" refers to penis, while "treasure" refers to the female genitalia.)

For some, this sonnet is the frank expression of the poet's sexual desire for the young man, and the addition of the "one thing" defeats the poet's procreative, but not his sexual, desire. Others see the sonnet as proof that the poet's lust for the young man is never consummated; women "use" the friend for sex, but the poet's love transcends physical gratification. He says, in effect, Give women your body; I'll take your mind. Incidentally, the pun on "pricked" has been blandly annotated "to mark" (which it does) but the word also refers to the "addition" that defeats the poet's intentions.

We'll probably never know Shakespeare's sexual preferences, though it's likely he was bisexual. He was fascinated by sexual ambiguity and the way in which one sex could behave like the other, and some of the most passionate relationships in the plays and poems are between men—Valentine and Proteus in *Two Gentlemen of Verona*, Antonio and Sebastian in *Twelfth Night*, Bassanio and Antonio in *The Merchant of Venice*, Iago and Othello in *Othello*, and Coriolanus and Aufidius in *Coriolanus*.

The Western ideal of romantic love, which traditionally refers to heterosexual desire, doesn't go very far in illuminating what Shakespeare means in the Sonnets. The poet uses a deceptively simple word, "love," to convey a complex range of emotions and objects. Viewed as a whole, the entire sequence is a full expression of the diverse ways human beings can love—homosexual, heterosexual, intellectual, companionable, paternal, the purely idealistic as well as the purely carnal. In some poems, the lover's agony is so closely aligned with his pleasure that the two are indistinguishable. To classify the Sonnets as either heterosexual or homosexual would be to oversimplify them, ignoring Shakespeare's great achievement.

The Words

"His words are a very fantastical banquet."
—*Much Ado About Nothing*, II,3,20

INTRODUCTION TO "COINED BY SHAKESPEARE"

by Jeffrey McQuain and Stanley Malless

William Shakespeare's reputation has never been greater. Almost four centuries after the playwright's death, his publications are thriving, his stage productions are multiplying, and films based on his plays are flourishing. Audience today may view stagings of the Bard's works by more than 150 companies and festivals around the world, from a summer festival in Williamsburg, Virginia, to a full season at the recently rebuilt Globe Theatre in London. Beyond this planet, the moons that circle Uranus have been given names of Shakespeare characters ranging from *Juliet* and *Ophelia* to *Oberon* and *Puck*. Underlining that universal success, a *Newsweek* headline at the end of 1996 nominated the playwright "Dead White Male of the Year," and *The Washington Post* named "Greatest Genius of the Millennium," adding a rhetorical "Any questions?"

Scholarship about Shakespeare has similarly soared. A 1983 bibliography for *Henry V*, for instance, listed more than 2,000 studies of that single play, including works written in Ukrainian and Korean. Last year a CD-ROM released by Cambridge University Press, covering Shakespeare scholarship from 1990 to 1993, provided more than 12,000 entries and "Shaksper," an electronic Shakespeare conference, now boasts more than 1,000 members worldwide. Here, however, is the first book ever to focus on the Bard's coinages.

How many words has Shakespeare added to English? Guesses have ranged from a few hundred terms to more than 10,000, with the most likely estimate approximately 1,500 words. As the scholar Marvin Spevack has commented, "Shakespeare's was the period of the most rapid growth of vocabulary in the recorded history of the language." Other writers of the English Renaissance also added to the language; the dramatist Ben Jonson, for instance, is credited with such words as *analytic* and *antagonist*. But it is Shakespeare, employing more than 20,000 words in his plays and poems, whose inventiveness and creative wordplay have most widely enriched our daily vocabulary.

Bardophiles and Bardophobes alike tend to think of Shakespeare's language all too often as an unfamiliar hodgepodge, ranging from oaths like *gadzooks* (meaning "God's hooks" and referring to the nails used in the Crucifixion) and *zounds* ("God's wounds") to archaisms like *bodkin* (a type of dagger) and *forsooth* ("truly").

The Brad's creations, however, reach far beyond the odd and the obsolete. From *assassination* to *zany,* these words are encountered every day. Cracker Barrel restaurants, for instance, offer "*Traditional* Favorites," Pontiac boasts, "We Build *Excitement*," and a recipe in *The New York Times Magazine* offers the perfect "*hint*: it's what you do after you flour and before you simmer."

Shakespeare's words are current in business (*employer* and *manager, investment* and *retirement*), as well as in law (*circumstantial* evidence and *foregone* conclusions) and politics (especially among those who *negotiate* or *petition*). The *advertising* world looks for new *designs* and *exposure.* Reporters profess familiarity with the word *reword,* if not with *misquote,* and activists actively use the Bard's best in phrases from "civil rights *protesters*" to "human rights *violations.*" The most romantic embrace such nouns as *courtship* and *embrace,* along with *engagement* and *never-ending* love, and animal lovers love the playwright's language, from *puppy dog* to *watchdog.*

Some of Shakespeare's choice words have remained commonplace (*skim milk* and *critic*), while others remain in the dictionary though they are rarely used (*consanguineous* and *kickshaw*). Examine enough of the Bard's coinages, however, and certain patterns begin to appear. Few words, in fact, emerge from a vacuum (although some words, such as *puke,* must remain labeled "origin unknown"); the majority develop from a handful of work-making practices.

First and foremost is functional shift, as Shakespeare change nouns into verbs (*film* and *champion*) or verbs into nouns (*dawn* and *scuffle*), verbs into adjectives (*hush*) or adjectives into nouns (*accused*). Another frequent practice is the adding of a prefix or a suffix to an existing word, from *eventful* to *remorseless.* Sometimes part of a word is subtracted by means of back-formation, leading to *impede* from *impediment.* Words derived from proper names proliferate, from the adjective *Promethean* to the noun *Xantippe* and the verb *pander,* derived from the name of Pandarus.

New meanings are given to old words. (To realize how meanings may change, note that *sharer* in Elizabethan times meant a stockholder in a theater company, and *housekeeper* was not a maid but a landlord of the theater building or "house.") Old words are also given new spellings by Shakespeare (*alligator*). Also frequent is compounding, the putting together of existing words, from the nouns *birthplace* and *eyeball* and the verb *undervalue*, to the adjectives *cold-blooded* and *softhearted* and the adverb *downstairs.*

Since his death in 1616, Shakespeare himself has fallen subject to neologizing. In 1896, George Bernard Shaw introduced *Shakespeare* as a verb meaning "to act in a Shakespeare play." Excessive worship of Shakespeare was first dismissed in 1864 as *Shakespearolatry,* spawning *Shakespearolaters* eleven years later. In 1903, Shaw coined the simpler *Bardolaters,* based on the Middle English *Bard,* "poet," which was first popularized as a title for Shakespeare by the eighteenth-century actor David Garrick. Six years after the introduction of Shaw's word, Mark Twain attacked the *Stratfordians* (as opposed to *Baconians* or *Oxfordians*), as well as Twain's dubious *Shakesperoids* for those who consider Shakespeare's words sacrosanct.

During the nineteenth century, Dr. Thomas Bowdler tried to rewrite those words. A "bowdlerized" edition, *The Family Shakespeare,* appeared in 1818, omitting "those words and expressions . . . which cannot with propriety be read aloud in the family." In this century, others have also rewritten the plays, ostensibly to simplify the words for modern understanding, although purists will argue that Hamlet's "Get thee to a nunnery" loses something in its translation to "Become a nun!"

Today the words of Shakespeare, coinages or not, have become fair game for advertisers and headline writers, who thrive on Shakespearean puns. As an affectionate tribute to the Bard, the cosmetics company Avon took its name from the river that flows through Stratford; less endearing is "Bubble, bubble, no toil or trouble" from a current commercial for a contact lens solution, echoing the Three Witches in *Macbeth*. Among recent headlines, "Now Is the Winter of Our Disc Content" in *Variety* plays upon the opening line of *Richard III*, and "Most Unkindest Glut of All" in *The Chronicle of Higher Education* lightly twists Mark Antony's words from *Julius Caesar*.

FROM
"ENTHUSIASMS"

by Bernard Levin

If you cannot understand my argument, and declare "It's Greek to me," you are quoting Shakespeare; if you claim to be more sinned against than sinning, you are quoting Shakespeare; if you recall your salad days, you are quoting Shakespeare; if you act more in sorrow than in anger, if your wish is father to the thought, if your lost property has vanished into thin air, you are quoting Shakespeare; if you have ever refused to budge an inch or suffered from green-eyed jealousy, if you have played fast and loose, if you have been tongue-tied, a tower of strength, hoodwinked or in a pickle, if you have knitted your brows, made a virtue of necessity, insisted on fair play, slept not one wink, stood on ceremony, danced attendance (on your lord and master), laughed yourself into stitches, had short shrift, cold comfort or too much of a good thing, if you have seen better days or lived in a fool's paradise—why, be that as it may, the more fool you, for it is a foregone conclusion that you are (as good luck would have it) quoting Shakespeare; if you think it is early days and clear out bag and baggage, if you think it is high time and that that is the long and short of it, if you believe that the game is up and that truth will out even if it involves your own flesh and blood, if you lie low till the crack of doom because you suspect foul play, if you have your teeth set on edge (at one fell swoop) without rhyme or reason, then—to give the devil his due—if the truth were known (for surely you have a tongue in your head) you are quoting Shakespeare; even if you bid me good riddance and send me packing, if you wish I were dead as a doornail, if you think I am an eyesore, a laughing stock, the devil incarnate, a stony-hearted villain, bloody-minded or a blinking idiot, then—by Jove! O Lord! Tut, tut! for goodness' sake! what the dickens! but me no buts—it is all one to me, for you are quoting Shakespeare.

NO-HOLDS BARD
A GLOSSARY OF SEXUAL SLANG
by Norrie Epstein

There's no denying it: Shakespeare was not merely bawdy—the usual terms used to convey full-blooded Elizabethan lustiness—he was stunningly vulgar. And his audience loved it. Bodily functions, secretions, smells, references that we would consider tasteless or private, were to them the pinnacle of wit. Privacy, particularly concerning personal hygiene, is a relatively modern idea, and the Elizabethans were far less squeamish than we are today.

Shakespeare, as might be expected, used bawdy language with more verve than his contemporaries, the most neutral words often doing overtime as double, and sometimes triple and even quadruple, entendres (for instance, Shakespeare was fond of the word "will," which variously meant sexual desire, penis, vagina, and was, of course, his own name). Once you know the Elizabethan meaning of one or two words, a whole passage suddenly takes on a startling alternative meaning. Slang hunting in Shakespeare is amusing, and the underlying crudity doesn't necessarily detract from the beauty of the lines—it only adds another dimension. What makes Shakespeare unique is that he is capable of being tender, sexy, funny, and sad, all at the same time.

Since most Elizabethan sexual slang is no longer current, students today can study *Romeo and Juliet* without any idea of what they're reading. Editors tend to evade explicit annotation, resorting to the bland "This is a bawdy quibble," the editorial equivalent of a squirm. This is unfortunate, since understanding Shakespeare's earthiness might enhance his reputation among high school students. Guardians of morality who complain of obscene lyrics in rock music are unaware that teenagers hear a lot worse in their English class, albeit uncomprehendingly. Given the explicit nature of Shakespeare's works, one wonders if he could have received an NEA grant had he applied today.

If you're curious—or just prurient—look at Frankie Rubinstein's *A Dictionary of Shakespeare's Sexual Puns and Their Significance* or Eric

Partridge's classic *Shakespeare Bawdy.*

Anatomical Humor: The Bard was not above the locker-room school of humor, as in this exchange from *The Comedy of Errors:*

> *Dromio.* She is spherical, like a globe. I could find out countries
>   in her.
> *Antipholus.* In what part of her body stands Ireland?
> *Dromio.* Marry, sir, in her buttocks. I found it out by the bogs.
>
> *Antipholus.* Where stood Belgia, the Netherlands?
> *Dromio.* O, sir, I did not look so low.
>
> (III,2,120-25,145-47)

("Bogs" was slang for the buttocks; Eric Partridge writes that "Belgia" is a pun on belly.)

Arise (or stand): To have an erection. Shakespeare belabors this word and its meaning in Sonnet 151: ". . . flesh stays [waits for] no farther reason / But, rising at thy name, doth point out thee / As his triumphant prize." ("Point" is another bawdy quibble, since it means, like "prick," to mark or point out and to rise.) In fact, the entire sonnet is an extended metaphor about the rise and fall of the flesh. When Titania tells Bottom "Arise, arise," she is not only telling him to wake up.

Banter (sexual): Perhaps the most famous sexual banter occurs in *The Taming of the Shrew:*

> *Petruchio.* Who knows not where a wasp does wear his sting?
>   In his tail.
> *Katherina.* In his tongue.
> *Petruchio.* Whose tongue?
> *Katherina .* Yours, if you talk of tails, and so farewell.
> *Petruchio.* What, with my tongue in your tail?
>
> (II,1,213-17)

Bottom: In *A Midsummer Night's Dream,* the word has a triple meaning: it is the name of a character; it means the buttocks, or ass, which is also a pun on the beast that Bottom is turned into; and the ass was regarded as the most well-endowed animal in the Elizabethan bestiary.

Cod: A common pun referring to the male organ. But anything to do with fish—of any species—was automatically suggestive and could start the audience laughing merely by association. (Mercutio upon seeing Romeo: "Here's Romeo without the roe.") The editor of the Folger Library edition of the comedies decorously defines "cod" as "strictly the husks containing the peas."

Codpiece: A fashionable item of clothing, resembling a jockstrap worn over a man's hose instead of beneath it.

Count: Often used for its similarity to the English vernacular for the female genitalia. When Hamlet, with his head on Ophelia's lap, tells her he is thinking of "country matters," he pointedly stresses the first syllable.

Die: Sexual intercourse or orgasm. The most common sexual pun in Elizabethan literature. According to Elizabethan physiology, each act of sexual intercourse shortened the lover's life by about a minute or so, owing to the discharge of "animal fluids." Thus, every orgasm was a miniature death. From *Antony and Cleopatra*:

> *Enobarbus.* Under a compelling occasion, let women die. It were a
>   pity to cast them away for nothing, though between them and
>   a great cause they should be esteemed nothing.
>
> (I,2,138-41)

Note how shrewdly Shakespeare slips in the double entendres. Women experience orgasm "under" something that compels them. "Nothing" was slang for sexual intercourse and the female genitalia. Between them and a "great cause" (a penis) lies nothing.

Double Entendres: Shakespeare's erotic poem "Venus and Adonis" proves that gorgeous lyrics are often the most suggestive:

> I'll be a park, and thou shalt be my deer:
> Feed where thou wilt, on mountain or in dale;
> Graze on my lips; and if those hills be dry,
> Stray lower, where the pleasant fountains lie.
>
> Within this limit is relief enough,
> Sweet bottom-grass and high delightful plain,
> Round rising hillocks, brakes obscure and rough . . .

Eric Partridge notes that "bottom-grass" referred to the "hair growing in and about the crotch," "brakes" was pubic hair; "groves" referred to the pubic area. According to Frankie Rubinstein, "grave" meant to roam freely, but it also suggested promiscuity. "Park" connoted a woman's genitals. It was commonplace to apply topographical terms to the female anatomy.

Green: Connoted virility and potency. See the scene in *Henry V* in which Falstaff's former mistress, the Hostess, relates her discovery of his death. You'll never read this scene in quite the same way again:

> . . . for after I saw him fumble with the sheets, and play with flowers, and smile upon his fingers' ends, I knew there was but one way; for his nose was as sharp as a pen, and 'a babbled of green fields. . . . I put my hand into the bed, and felt them [his feet], and they were as cold as any stone; then I felt to his knees, and so up'ard, and up'ard, and all was as cold as any stone.
>
> (II,3,13-25)

Rubinstein annotates "flowers" and "nose" as penis; "green fields" suggested virility; "stone" was a common word for testicle. The Hostess mourns her old lover's death—both his literal end and his last erection. This speech, which unites a genuine elegiac tone with masturbatory imagery, is something few poets could get away with. Given Falstaff's earthiness and his role in the play as a symbol of the flesh, it's fitting that the Hostess can tell he's dead only by feeling his penis. The two sensibilities, the bawdy and the sentimental, don't cancel each other out; in fact, surprisingly, each enhances the other.

Hell: Slang often used in passages of sexual nausea to indicate a woman's genitals. See Sonnet 144, in which the poet suspects the friend of being inside the Dark Lady's hell.

Leaping House: A brothel.

Naught: Wickedness, with implications of sexual intercourse—usually adulterous. From *Richard III*:

> *Brackenbury.* With this, my lord, myself have naught to do.
> *Richard.* Naught to do with Mistress Shore? I tell thee, fellow,
>   He that doth naught with her, excepting one,

Were best he do it secretly, alone.

(I,1,97-100)

Pricks and Bowls: Pricks referred to a game of archery, bowls to bowling, but both words are frequently used to suggest other games. According to Rubinstein, games were often metaphors for sex. From *Love's Labour's Lost*:

> *Costard.* She is too hard for you at pricks, sir. Challenge her to
> bowl.
> *Boyet.* I fear too much rubbing.

(IV,1,139-40)

Quaint, Queynt, or Coynt: Female genitalia. When a man said he "made" a woman's "acqueyntaince," he meant that he knew her very well indeed. The word refers to the vernacular "cunt" and has undergone an interesting etymological evolution. At first, in addition to its anatomical meaning, it referred to something dark, secretive, and curiously wrought. It's a linguist's—or a psychiatrist's—task to figure out why, but through the ages the word has slowly been purged of its covert meanings, until now it refers to the opposite of its original definition: "quaint" now means something dainty, sweetly picturesque, and old-fashioned.

Seduction: Falstaff to Mrs. Ford in *The Merry Wives of Windsor*: "Let the sky rain potatoes. Let it thunder to the tune of 'Greensleeves,' hail kissing-comfits and snow eringoes. Let there come a tempest of provocation, I will shelter me here." (V,5,18-21) (One wonders where Falstaff is pointing.) Potatoes, kissing-comfits (perfumed sweetmeats), and snow eringoes (sea holly) were believed to have aphrodisiacal properties; "provocation" meant sexual stimulation; the popular song "Greensleeves" was probably the Elizabethan equivalent to "Bolero" or Johnny Mathis, standard seduction fare.

Thing: A penis. Rosalind and Orlando's seemingly innocent banter in *As You Like It* is filled with double entendres:

> *Rosalind.* Are you not good?
> *Orlando.* I hope so.
> *Rosalind.* Why then, can one desire too much of a good thing?

(IV,1,110-12)

THE QPB COMPANION TO SHAKESPEARE

Whore: Elizabethan English had dozens of words to describe a prostitute, and Shakespeare seems to have used them all: beef, wench, jade, baggage, punk, slut, Winchester goose, taffeta punk, guinea-hen, bawd, quean, laced mutton, fish, stale, and doxy. (Prostitutes often dressed in taffeta; the bishop of Winchester owned the land where most of the brothels were located, and prostitutes had to pay him revenue out of their earnings; hence they were like geese, kept and fattened by the church.)

Will: Not only a pun on Shakespeare's name, but also a reference to sexual desire, as well as the male and female genitals. Shakespeare exploits the word to the maximum, particularly in Sonnet 135, where it occurs twelve times in fourteen lines:

> Wilt thou, whose will is large and spacious,
> Not once vouchsafe to hide my will in thine?

According to the novelist Anthony Burgess, this sonnet is a "hymn to the male thrust." When the poet learns that the lady has been sleeping with three men named Will, he cynically observes in Sonnet 136 that all these Wills have fulfilled—and filled—the lady's will: "Ay, fill it full with wills."

The Critics

"I am nothing if not critical."

—*Othello*, II,1,117

SHAKESPEARE'S UNIVERSALISM
by Harold Bloom

The answer to the question "Why Shakespeare?" must be "Who else is there?"

Romantic criticism, from Hazlitt through Pater and A. C. Bradley on to Harold Goddard, taught that what matters most in Shakespeare is shared by him more with Chaucer and with Dostoevsky than with his contemporaries Marlowe and Ben Jonson. Inner selves do not exactly abound in the works of the creators of Tamburlaine and of Sir Epicure Mammon. Providing contexts that Shakespeare shared with George Chapman or Thomas Middleton will never tell you why Shakespeare, rather than Chapman or Middleton, changed us. Of all critics, Dr. Johnson best conveys the singularity of Shakespeare. Dr. Johnson first saw and said where Shakespeare's eminence was located: in a diversity of persons. No one, before or since Shakespeare, made so many separate selves.

Thomas Carlyle, dyspeptic Victorian prophet, must now be the least favored of all Shakespeare critics who once were respected. And yet the most useful single sentence about Shakespeare is his: "If called to define Shakespeare's faculty, I should say superiority of Intellect, and think I had included all under that." Carlyle was merely accurate; there are great poets who are not thinkers, like Tennyson and Walt Whitman, and great poets of shocking conceptual originality, like Blake and Emily Dickinson. But no Western writer, or any Eastern author I am able to read, is equal to Shakespeare as an intellect, and among writers I would include the principal philosophers, the religious sages, and the psychologists from Montaigne through Nietzsche to Freud.

This judgment, whether Carlyle's or mine, scarcely seems Bardolatry to me; perhaps it only repeats T. S. Eliot's observation that all we can hope for is to be wrong about Shakespeare in a new way. I propose only that we cease to be wrong about him by stopping trying to be right. I have read and taught Shakespeare almost daily for these past twelve years, and am certain that I see him only darkly. His intellect is superior to mine: why should I not learn to interpret him by gauging that superiority, which after all is the only answer to "Why Shakespeare?" Our supposed advances in cultural anthropology or in other modes of "Theory" are not advances upon *him*.

In learning, intellect, and personality, Samuel Johnson still seems to me first among all Western literary critics. His writings on Shakespeare necessarily have a unique value: the foremost of interpreters commenting upon the largest of all authors cannot fail to be of permanent use and interest. For Johnson, the essence of poetry was *invention*, and only Homer could be Shakespeare's rival in originality. Invention, in Johnson's sense as in ours, is a process of finding, or of finding out. We owe Shakespeare everything, Johnson says, and means that Shakespeare has taught us to understand human nature. Johnson does not go so far as to say that Shakespeare invented us, but he does intimate the true tenor of Shakespearean mimesis: "Imitations produce pain or pleasure, not because they are mistaken for realities, but because they bring realities to mind." An experiential critic above all, Johnson knew that realities change, indeed *are* change. What Shakespeare invents are ways of representing human changes, alterations not only caused by flaws and by decay but effected by the will as well, and by the will's temporal vulnerabilities. One way of defining Johnson's vitality as a critic is to note the consistent power of his inferences: he is always sufficiently *inside* Shakespeare's plays to judge them as he judges human life, without ever forgetting that Shakespeare's function is to bring life to mind, to make us aware of what we could not find without Shakespeare. Johnson knows that Shakespeare is not life, that Falstaff and Hamlet are larger than life, but Johnson knows also that Falstaff and Hamlet have altered life. Shakespeare, according to Johnson, justly imitates *essential* human nature, which is a universal and not a social phenomenon. A. D. Nuttall, in his admirably Johnsonian *A New Mimesis* (1983), suggested that Shakespeare, like Chaucer, "implicitly contested the transcendentalist conception of reality." Johnson, firmly Christian, would not allow himself to say that, but he clearly understood it, and his uneasiness underlies his shock at the murder of Cordelia at the end of *King Lear*.

Only the Bible has a circumference that is everywhere, like Shakespeare's, and most people who read the Bible regard it as divinely inspired, if not indeed supernaturally composed. The Bible's center is God, or perhaps the vision or idea of God, whose location necessarily is unfixed. Shakespeare's works have been termed the secular Scripture, or more simply the fixed center of the Western canon. What the Bible and Shakespeare have in common actually is rather less than most people suppose, and I myself suspect that the common element is only a certain universalism, global and multicultural. Universalism is now not much in fashion, except in religious institutions and those they strongly influence. Yet I hardly see how one can begin to consider Shakespeare without finding some way to account for his pervasive presence in the most unlikely contexts: here, there, and everywhere at once. He is a system of northern lights, an aurora borealis visible where most of us will never go. Libraries and playhouses (and cinemas) cannot contain him; he has become a spirit or "spell of light," almost too vast to apprehend. High Romantic Bardolatry, now so much disdained in our self-defiled academies, is merely the most normative of the faiths that worship him.

I am not concerned, in this book, with how this happened, but with why it continues. If any author has become a mortal god, it must be Shakespeare. Who can dispute his good eminence, to which merit alone raised him? Poets and scholars revere Dante; James Joyce and T. S. Eliot would have liked to prefer him to Shakespeare, yet could not. Common readers, and thankfully we still possess them, rarely can read Dante; yet they can read and attend Shakespeare. His few peers—Homer, the Yahwist, Dante, Chaucer, Cervantes, Tolstoy, perhaps Dickens—remind us that the representation of human character and personality remains always the supreme literary value, whether in drama, lyric, or narrative. I am naïve enough to read incessantly because I cannot, on my own, get to know enough people profoundly enough. Shakespeare's own playgoers preferred Falstaff and Hamlet to all his other characters, and so do we, because Fat Jack and the Prince of Denmark manifest the most comprehensive consciousnesses in all of literature, larger than those of the biblical J Writer's Yahweh, of the Gospel of Mark's Jesus, of Dante the Pilgrim and Chaucer the Pilgrim, of Don Quixote and Esther Summerson, of Proust's narrator and Leopold Bloom. Perhaps indeed it is Falstaff and Hamlet, rather than Shakespeare, who are mortal gods, or perhaps the greatest of wits and the greatest of intellects between them divinized their creator.

What do Falstaff and Hamlet most closely share? If the question can be answered, we might get inside the man Shakespeare, whose personal mystery, for us, is that he seems not at all mysterious to us. Setting mere morality aside, Falstaff and Hamlet palpably are superior to everyone else whom they, and we, encounter in their plays. This superiority is cognitive, linguistic, and imaginative, but most vitally it is a matter of personality. Falstaff and Hamlet are the greatest of charismatics: they embody the Blessing, in its prime Yahwistic sense of "more life into a time without boundaries" (to appropriate from myself). Heroic vitalists are not larger than life; they are life's largeness. Shakespeare, who seems never to have made heroic or vitalistic gestures in his daily life, produced Falstaff and Hamlet as art's tribute to nature. More even than all the other Shakespearean prodigies— Rosalind, Shylock, Iago, Lear, Macbeth, Cleopatra—Falstaff and Hamlet are the invention of the human, the inauguration of personality as we have come to recognize it.

The idea of Western character, of the self as a moral agent, has many sources: Homer and Plato, Aristotle and Sophocles, the Bible and St. Augustine, Dante and Kant, and all you might care to add. Personality, in our sense, is a Shakespearean invention, and is not only Shakespeare's greatest originality but also the authentic cause of his perpetual pervasiveness. Insofar as we ourselves value, and deplore, our own personalities, we are the heirs of Falstaff and of Hamlet, and of all the other persons who throng Shakespeare's theater of what might be called the colors of the spirit.

How skeptical Shakespeare himself may have been of the value of personality, we cannot know. For Hamlet, the self is an abyss, the chaos of virtual nothingness. For Falstaff, the self is everything. Perhaps Hamlet, in Act V, transcends his own nihilism; we cannot be certain, in that ambiguous slaughter that reduces the court at Elsinore to the fop Osric, a few extras, and the inside outsider, Horatio. Is Hamlet self-divested of all his ironies at the end? Why does he give his dying vote to the bully boy Fortinbras, who wastes soldiers' lives in a battle for a barren bit of ground scarcely wide enough to bury their corpses? Falstaff, rejected and destroyed, remains an image of exuberance. His sublime personality, a vast value for us, has not saved him from the hell of betrayed and misplaced affection, and yet our final vision of him, related by Mistress Quickly in *Henry V*, remains a supreme value, evoking the Twenty-third Psalm and a child at play with flowers. It seems odd to observe that Shakespeare gives his two greatest personalities the oxymoron we call "a good death," but how else could we phrase it?

Are there *personalities* (in our sense) in the plays of any of Shakespeare's rivals? Marlowe deliberately kept to cartoons, even in Barabas, wickedest of Jews, and Ben Jonson as deliberately confined himself to ideograms, even in Volpone, whose final punishment so saddens us. I have a great taste for John Webster, but his heroines and villains alike vanish when juxtaposed to those of Shakespeare. Scholars attempt to impress upon us the dramatic virtues of George Chapman and of Thomas Middleton, but no one suggests that either of them could endow a role with human inwardness. It provokes considerable resistance from scholars when I say that Shakespeare invented us, but it would be a statement of a different order if anyone were to assert that our personalities would be different if Jonson and Marlowe had never written. Shakespeare's wonderful joke was to have his Ancient Pistol, Falstaff's follower in *Henry IV, Part Two,* identify himself with Marlowe's Tamburlaine; much slyer was Shakespeare's ironic yet frightening portrait of Marlowe as Edmund, the brilliantly seductive villain of *King Lear*. Malvolio in *Twelfth Night* is both a parodistic portrait of Ben Jonson and a personality so humanly persuasive as to remind the playgoer, unforgettably, that Jonson has no fully human beings in his own plays. Shakespeare, not only witty in himself but the cause of wit in other men, absorbed his rivals in order to hint that their own extraordinary personalities far surpassed *their* creations, but not what Shakespeare could make of them. And yet Edmund's nihilistic intellect, like Iago's, is dwarfed by Hamlet's, and Malvolio's uneasily comic splendor is a teardrop alongside the cosmological ocean of Falstaff's laughter. We perhaps are too attentive to Shakespeare's theatrical metaphors, to his overt self-awareness as an actor-playwright. His models must have come more frequently from other spheres than his own, yet he may not have been "imitating life" but creating it, in most of his finest work.

What made his art of characterization possible? How can you create beings who are "free artists of themselves," as Hegel called Shakespeare's personages? Since Shakespeare, the best answer might be: "By an imitation of Shakespeare." It cannot be said that Shakespeare imitated Chaucer and the Bible in the sense that he imitated Marlowe and Ovid. He took hints from Chaucer, and they were more important than his Marlovian and Ovidian origins, at least once he had reached the creation of Falstaff. There are traces aplenty of fresh human personalities in Shakespeare before Falstaff: Faulconbridge the Bastard in *King John,* Mercutio in *Romeo and Juliet,* Bottom in *A Midsummer Night's Dream.* And there is Shylock, at once a fabulous monster, the Jew incarnate, and also a troubling human uneasily joined with the monster in an uncanny blend. But there is a difference in kind between even these and Hamlet, and only a difference in degree between Falstaff and Hamlet. Inwardness becomes the heart of light and of darkness in ways more radical than literature previously could sustain.

Shakespeare's uncanny power in the rendering of personality is perhaps beyond explanation. Why do his personages seem so *real* to us, and how could he contrive that illusion so persuasively? Historical (and historicized) considerations have not aided us much in the answering of such questions. Ideals, both societal and individual, were perhaps more prevalent in Shakespeare's world than they appear to be in ours. Leeds Barroll notes that Renaissance ideals, whether Christian or philosophical or occult, tended to emphasize our need to join something personal that yet was larger than ourselves, God or a spirit. A certain strain or anxiety ensued, and Shakespeare became the greatest master at exploiting the void between persons and the personal ideal. Did his invention of what we recognize as "personality" result from that exploitation? Certainly we hear Shakespeare's influence upon his disciple John Webster, when Webster's Flamineo, dying at the close of *The White Devil,* cries out:

While we look up to heaven we confound
Knowledge with knowledge.

In Webster, even at his best, we can hear the Shakespearean paradoxes ably repeated, but the speakers have no individuality. Who can tell us the personality differences, in *The White Devil*, between Flamineo and Lodovico? Looking up to heaven and confounding knowledge with knowledge do not save Flamineo and Lodovico from being names upon a page. Hamlet, perpetually arguing with himself, does not seem to owe his overwhelming reality to a confounding of personal and ideal knowledge. Rather, Shakespeare gives us a Hamlet who is an agent, rather than an effect, of clashing realizations. We are convinced of Hamlet's superior reality because Shakespeare has made Hamlet free by making him know the truth, truth too intolerable for us to endure. A Shakespearean audience is like the gods in Homer: we look on and listen, and are not tempted to intervene. But we also are unlike the audience constituted by Homer's gods; being mortal, we too confound knowledge with knowledge. We cannot extract, from Shakespeare's era or from our own, social information that will explain his ability to create "forms more real than living men," as Shelley phrased it. Shakespeare's rival playwrights were subject to the same disjunctions between ideas of love, order, and the Eternal as he was, but they gave us eloquent caricatures, at best, rather than men and women.

We cannot know, by reading Shakespeare and seeing him played, whether he had any extrapoetic beliefs or disbeliefs. G. K. Chesterton, a wonderful literary critic, insisted that Shakespeare was a Catholic dramatist, and that Hamlet was more orthodox than skeptical. Both assertions seem to me quite unlikely, yet I do not know, and Chesterton did not know either. Christopher Marlowe had his ambiguities and Ben Jonson his ambivalences, but sometimes we can hazard surmises as to their personal stances. By reading Shakespeare, I can gather that he did not like lawyers, preferred drinking to eating, and evidently lusted after both genders. But I certainly do not have a clue as to whether he favored Protestantism or Catholicism or neither, and I do not know whether he believed or disbelieved in God or in resurrection. His politics, like his religion, evades me, but I think he was too wary to have any. He sensibly was afraid of mobs and of uprisings, yet he was afraid of authority also. He aspired after gentility, rued having been an actor, and might seem to have valued *The Rape of Lucrece* over *King Lear*, a judgment in which he remains outrageously unique (except, perhaps, for Tolstoy).

Chesterton and Anthony Burgess both stressed Shakespeare's vitality; I would go a touch farther and call Shakespeare a vitalist, like his own Falstaff. Vitalism, which William Hazlitt called "gusto," may be the ultimate clue to

Shakespeare's preternatural ability to endow his personages with personalities and with utterly individuated styles of speaking. I scarcely can believe that Shakespeare preferred Prince Hal to Falstaff, as most scholars opine. Hal is a Machiavel; Falstaff, like Ben Jonson himself (and like Shakespeare?), is rammed with life. So, of course, are the great Shakespearean murderous villains: Aaron the Moor, Richard III, Iago, Edmund, Macbeth. So indeed are the comic villains: Shylock, Malvolio, and Caliban. Exuberance, well-nigh apocalyptic in its fervor, is as marked in Shakespeare as it is in Rabelais, Blake, and Joyce. The man Shakespeare, affable and shrewd, was no more Falstaff than he was Hamlet, and yet something in his readers and playgoers perpetually associates the dramatist with both figures. Only Cleopatra and the strongest of the villains—Iago, Edmund, Macbeth—hold on in our memories with the staying force of Falstaff's insouciance and Hamlet's intellectual intensity.

In reading Shakespeare's plays, and to a certain extent in attending their performances, the merely sensible procedure is to immerse yourself in the text and its speakers, and allow your understanding to move outward from what you read, hear, and see to whatever contexts suggest themselves as relevant. That was the procedure from the times of Dr. Johnson and David Garrick, of William Hazlitt and Edmund Kean, through the eras of A. C. Bradley and Henry Irving, of G. Wilson Knight and John Gielgud. Alas, sensible, even "natural" as this way was, it is now out of fashion, and has been replaced by arbitrary and ideologically imposed contextualization, the staple of our bad time. In "French Shakespeare" (as I shall go on calling it), the procedure is to begin with a political stance all your own, far out and away from Shakespeare's plays, and then to locate some marginal bit of English Renaissance social history that seems to sustain your stance. Social fragment in hand, you move in from outside upon the poor play, and find some connection, however established, between your supposed social fact and Shakespeare's words. It would cheer me to be persuaded that I am parodying the operations of the professors and directors of what I call "Resentment"— those critics who value theory over the literature itself—but I have given a plain account of the going thing, whether in the classroom or on the stage.

Substituting the name of "Shakespeare" for that of "Jesus," I am moved to cite William Blake:

> I am sure this Shakespeare will not do
> Either for Englishman or Jew.

What is inadequate about "French Shakespeare" is hardly that it is not "English Shakespeare," let alone Jewish, Christian, or Islamic Shakespeare:

most simply, it is just not Shakespeare, who does not fit very easily into Foucault's "archives" and whose energies were not primarily "social." You can bring absolutely anything to Shakespeare and the plays will light it up, far more than what you bring will illuminate the plays. Though professional resenters insist that the aesthetic stance is itself an ideology, I scarcely agree, and I bring nothing but the aesthetic (in Walter Pater's and Oscar Wilde's language) to Shakespeare in this book. Or rather, he brings it to me, since Shakespeare educated Pater, Wilde, and the rest of us in the aesthetic, which, as Pater observed, is an affair of perceptions and sensations. Shakespeare teaches us how and what to perceive, and he also instructs us how and what to sense and then to experience as sensation. Seeking as he did to enlarge us, not as citizens or as Christians but as consciousnesses, Shakespeare outdid all his preceptors as an entertainer. Our resenters, who can be described (without malice) as gender-and-power freaks, are not much moved by the plays as entertainment.

Though G. K. Chesterton liked to think that Shakespeare was a Catholic, at least in spirit, Chesterton was too good a critic to locate Shakespeare's universalism in Christianity. We might learn from that not to shape Shakespeare by our own cultural politics. Comparing Shakespeare with Dante, Chesterton emphasized Dante's spaciousness in dealing with Christian love and Christian liberty, whereas Shakespeare "was a pagan; in so far that he is at his greatest in describing great spirits in chains." Those "chains" manifestly are not political. They return us to universalism, to Hamlet above all, greatest of all spirits, thinking his way to the truth, of which he perishes. The ultimate use of Shakespeare is to let him teach you to think too well, to whatever truth you can sustain without perishing.

2

It is not an illusion that readers (and playgoers) find more vitality both in Shakespeare's words and in the characters who speak them than in any other author, perhaps in all other authors put together. Early modern English was shaped by Shakespeare: the *Oxford English Dictionary* is made in his image. Later modern human beings are still being shaped by Shakespeare, not as Englishmen, or as American women, but in modes increasingly postnational and postgender. He has become the first universal author, replacing the Bible in the secularized consciousness. Attempts to historicize his ascendancy continue to founder upon the uniqueness of his eminence, for the cultural factors critics find relevant to Shakespeare are precisely as relevant to Thomas Dekker and to George Chapman. Newfangled expositions of

Shakespeare do not persuade us, because their implicit program involves diminishing the difference between Shakespeare and the likes of Chapman.

What does not work, pragmatically, is any critical or theatrical fashion that attempts to assimilate Shakespeare to contexts, whether historical or here-and-now. Demystification is a weak technique to exercise upon the one writer who truly seems to have become himself only by representing other selves. I paraphrase Hazlitt upon Shakespeare; as the subtitle of this book ["Invention of the Human"] indicates, I happily follow in Hazlitt's wake, seeking the Shakespearean difference, that which overcomes all demarcations between cultures, or within cultures. What allowed Shakespeare to be the supreme *magister ludi*? Nietzsche, like Montaigne a psychologist almost of Shakespeare's power, taught that pain is the authentic origin of human memory. Since Shakespeare is the most memorable of writers, there may be a valid sense in which the pain Shakespeare affords us is as significant as the pleasure. One need not be Dr. Johnson to dread reading, or attending a performance of, *King Lear*, particularly Act V, where Cordelia is murdered, and where Lear dies, holding her corpse in his arms. I myself dread *Othello* even more; its painfulness exceeds all measure, provided that we (and the play's director) grant to Othello his massive dignity and value that alone make his degradation so terrible.

I cannot solve the puzzle of the representation of Shylock or even of Prince Hal/King Henry V. Primal ambivalence, popularized by Sigmund Freud, remains central to Shakespeare, and to a scandalous extent was Shakespeare's own invention. Memorable pain, or memory engendered through pain, ensues from an ambivalence both cognitive and affective, an ambivalence that we associate most readily with Hamlet but that is prepared by Shylock. Perhaps Shylock began as a farcical villain—I once believed this, but now I rather doubt it. The play is Portia's, and not Shylock's, but Shylock is the first of Shakespeare's internalized hero-villains, as contrasted with such externalized forerunners as Aaron the Moor and Richard III. I take it that Prince Hal/Henry V is the next abyss of inwardness after Shylock, and so another hero-villain, a pious and patriotic Machiavel, but the piety and the kingly quality are modifiers, while the hypocrisy is the substantive. Even so, the tenacious and justice-seeking Shylock essentially is a would-be slaughterer, and Shakespeare painfully persuades us that Portia, another delightful hypocrite, prevents an atrocity through her shrewdness. One would hope that *The Merchant of Venice* is painful even for Gentiles, though the hope may be illusory.

What is not illusory is the frightening power of Shylock's will, his demand to have his bond. One surely can speak of the frightening power of Hal/Henry V's will, his demand to have his throne, and France, and absolute sway over everyone, including their hearts and minds. Hamlet's greatness, his transcending of the hero-villain's role, has much to do with his rejection of the will, including the will to avenge, a project he evades by negation, in him a revisionary mode that reduces every context to theater. Shakespeare's theatrical genius is less Iago than Hamlet. Iago is nothing if not critical, but he is, at most, a great criminal-aesthete, and his insight fails him utterly in regard to Emilia, his own wife. Hamlet is much the freer artist, whose insight cannot fail, and who converts his mousetrap into Theater of the World. Where Shylock is an obsessive, and Hal/Henry V an ingrate who fails to see Falstaff's uniqueness, and even Iago never quite gets beyond a sense of the injured self (his own passed-over military virtue), Hamlet consciously takes on the burden of the theater's mystery as augmented by Shakespeare's strength. Hamlet, too, ceases to represent himself and becomes something other than a single self—a something that is a universal figure and not a picnic of selves. Shakespeare became unique by representing other humans; Hamlet is the difference that Shakespeare achieved. I am not suggesting that Hamlet's beautiful disinterestedness in Act V ever was or became one of Shakespeare's personal qualities, but rather that Hamlet's final stance personifies Shakespeare's Negative Capability, as John Keats termed it. At the end, Hamlet is no longer a real personage condemned to suffer inside a play, and the wrong play at that. The personage and the play dissolve into each other, until we have only the cognitive music of "let be" and "Let it be."

3

It is difficult to describe Shakespeare's modes of representation without resorting to oxymorons, since most of these modes are founded upon seeming contradictions. A "naturalistic unreality" suggests itself, to meet Wittgenstein's annoyed comment that life is *not* like Shakespeare. Owen Barfield replied to Wittgenstein in advance (1928):

> . . . there is a very real sense, humiliating as it may seem, in which what we generally venture to call *our* feelings are really Shakespeare's "meaning."

Life itself has become a naturalistic unreality, partly, because of Shakespeare's prevalence. To have invented our feelings is to have gone beyond psychologizing us: Shakespeare made us theatrical, even if we never attend a performance or read a play. After Hamlet literally has stopped the play—to joke about the War of the Theaters, to command the Player King to enact the absurd scene in which Aeneas recounts Priam's slaughter, to admonish the players to a little discipline—we more than ever regard Hamlet as *one of us*, somehow dropped into a role in a play, and the wrong play at that. The prince alone is real; the others, and all the action, constitute theater.

Can we conceive of ourselves without Shakespeare? By "ourselves" I do not mean only actors, directors, teachers, critics, but also you and everyone you know. Our education, in the English-speaking world, but in many other nations as well, has been Shakespearean. Even now, when our education has faltered, and Shakespeare is battered and truncated by our fashionable ideologues, the ideologues themselves are caricatures of Shakespearean energies. Their supposed "politics" reflect the passions of *his* characters, and insofar as they themselves possess any social energies, their secret sense of the societal is oddly Shakespearean. I myself would prefer them to be Machiavels and resenters on the Marlovian model of Barabas, Jew of Malta, but alas, their actual ideological paradigms are Iago and Edmund.

Do Shakespeare's modes of representation *in themselves* betray any ideological turn, whether Christian, skeptical, hermetic, or whatever? The question, difficult to frame, remains urgent in its implications: Is Shakespeare, in his plays, ultimately a celebrant of life, beyond tragedy, or is he pragmatically nihilistic? Since I myself am a heretical transcendentalist, gnostic in orientation, I would be happiest with a Shakespeare who seemed to hold on to at least a secular transcendence, a vision of the sublime. That seems not altogether true; the authentic Shakespearean litany chants variations upon the word "nothing," and the uncanniness of nihilism haunts almost every play, even the great, relatively unmixed comedies. As a playwright, Shakespeare seems too wise to believe *anything*, and while he seems to know not less than everything, he is careful to keep that knowing several steps short of transcendence. Since his eloquence is comprehensive, and his dramatic concern almost unfaltering, one cannot assign precedence even to the plays' apparent nihilism, and to their clear sense of nature's indifference, alike, to human codes and to human suffering. Still, the nihilism has a peculiar reverberation. We remember Leontes in *The Winter's Tale* hardly at all for his closing repentance—"Both your pardons, / That e'er I put between your holy looks / My ill suspicion"—but for his great paean of "nothings":

> Is this nothing?
> Why then the world and all that's in't, is nothing,
> The covering sky is nothing, Bohemia nothing,
> My wife is nothing, nor nothing have these nothings,
> If this be nothing.

His nihilizing madness matters to us, and his restored sanity does not, since true poetry indeed is of the Devil's party, in William Blake's dialectical sense of the Devil. Nahum Tate's sanitized *King Lear*, with its happy ending of Cordelia married to Edgar, and Lear benignly beaming upon his daughter and his godson, cheered up Dr. Johnson but deprives us of the *kenoma*, the sensible emptiness or waste land in which the actual play by William Shakespeare concludes.

4

Few among us are qualified to testify as to whether God is dead, or alive, or wandering somewhere in exile (the possibility I tend to favor). Some authors indeed are dead, but not William Shakespeare. As for dramatic characters, I never know how to take the assurances (and remonstrances) I receive from Shakespeare's current critics, who tell me that Falstaff, Hamlet, Rosalind, Cleopatra, and Iago are roles for actors and actresses but not "real people." Impressed as I (sometimes) am by these admonitions, I struggle always with the palpable evidence that my chastisers not only are rather less interesting than Falstaff and Cleopatra, but also are less persuasively alive than Shakespearean figures, who are (to steal from Ben Jonson) "rammed with life." When I was a child, and saw Ralph Richardson play Falstaff, I was so profoundly affected that I could never see Richardson again, on stage or on screen, without identifying him with Falstaff, despite this actor's extraordinary and varied genius. The reality of Falstaff has never left me, and a half century later was the starting point for this book. If a poor player struts and frets his hour upon the stage, and then is heard no more, we can say that a great player reverberates for a lifetime, most particularly if he acts not only a strong role, but a character deeper than life, a wit unmatched by anyone merely real whom we will ever know.

We ought to get these matters the right way round; *we* are not here to make moral judgments concerning Falstaff. Shakespeare perspectivizes his dramas so that, measure for measure, we are judged even as we attempt to judge. If your Falstaff is a roistering coward, a wastrel confidence man, an uncourted jester to Prince Hal, well, then, we know something of you, but we know no more about Falstaff. If your Cleopatra is an aging whore, and her Antony a would-be Alexander in his dotage, then we know a touch more about you and rather less about them than we should. Hamlet's players hold the mirror up to nature, but Shakespeare's is a mirror within a mirror, and both are mirrors with many voices. Falstaff, Hamlet, Cleopatra, and the rest are not images of voice (as lyric poets can be), and they do not speak either for Shakespeare or for nature. An art virtually unlimited, Shakespearean representation offers us neither nature nor a second nature, neither cosmos nor heterocosm. "The art itself is nature" (*The Winter's Tale*) is a wonderfully ambiguous declaration. If I am right in finding true Shakespearean character first in Faulconbridge the Bastard in *King John* and last in *The Tempest*, that still sets aside superb plays with a very different sort of characterization, ranging from the perplexed triad of *Troilus and Cressida, All's Well That Ends Well*, and *Measure for Measure* on to the hieratic figures of *The Two Noble Kinsmen*. That is to say, Shakespearean characterization is finally so varied that we cannot call any one mode of it "true."

5

Pragmatically there is little difference between speaking of "Hamlet as a character" and "Hamlet as a role for an actor." Yet, mostly because of the peculiarities of modern criticism, the time has come around when it seems salutory to speak again of "literary and dramatic character" in order better to comprehend Shakespeare's men and women. Very little is gained by reminding us that Hamlet is made up of and by words, that he is "just" a grouping of marks upon a page. "Character" means both a letter of the alphabet, and also ethos, a person's habitual way of life. Literary and dramatic character is an imitation of human character, or so we once thought, on the premise that words were as much like people as they were like things. Words of course refer to other words, but their impact upon us emanates, as Martin Price says, from the empiric realm where we live, and where we attribute values and meanings, to our ideas of persons. Such attributions are a kind of fact, and so are our impressions that some literary and dramatic characters reinforce our ideas of persons and some do not.

There are two contradictory ways to account for Shakespeare's eminence. If, for you, literature is primarily language, then the primacy of Shakespeare is only a cultural phenomenon, produced by sociopolitical urgencies. In this view, Shakespeare did not write Shakespeare—his plays were written by the social, political, and economic energies of his age. But so was everything else, then and now, because certain more or less recent Parisian speculators have convinced many (if not most) academic critics that there are no authors anyway.

The other way of exploring Shakespeare's continued supremacy is rather more empirical: he has been universally judged to be a more adequate representer of the universe of fact than anyone else, before him or since. This judgment has been dominant since at least the mid-eighteenth century; it has been staled by repetition, yet it remains merely true, banal as resentful theorists find it to be. We keep returning to Shakespeare because we need him; no one else gives us so much of the world most of us take to be fact. But in the book that follows, I will not just begin with the assumption that Shakespeare palpably was much the best writer we ever will know. Shakespeare's originality in the representation of character will be demonstrated throughout, as will the extent to which we all of use were, to a shocking degree, pragmatically reinvented by Shakespeare. Our ideas as to what makes the self authentically human owe more to Shakespeare than ought to be possible, but then he has become a Scripture, not to be read as many of us read the Bible or the Koran or Joseph Smith's Doctrines and Covenants, but also not be read as we read Cervantes or Dickens or Walt Whitman. *The Complete Works of William Shakespeare* could as soon be called *The Book of Reality*, fantastic as so much of Shakespeare deliberately intends to be. I have written elsewhere that Shakespeare is not only in himself the Western canon; he has become the universal canon, perhaps the only one that can survive the current debasement of our teaching institutions, here and abroad. Every other great writer may fall away, to be replaced by the anti-elitist swamp of Cultural Studies. Shakespeare will abide, even if he were to be expelled by the academics, in itself most unlikely. He extensively informs the language we speak, his principal characters have become our mythology, and he, rather than his involuntary follower Freud, is our psychologist. His persuasiveness has its unfortunate aspects; *The Merchant of Venice* may have been more of an incitement to anti-Semitism than *The Protocols of the Learned Elders of Zion*, though less than the Gospel of John. We pay a price for what we gain from Shakespeare.

"BETTER THAN SHAKESPEAR?"

by George Bernard Shaw

As to the other plays in this volume [this originally appeared as the preface to *Caesar and Cleopatra* in a volume called *Three Plays for Puritans*], the application of my title is less obvious, since neither Julius Caesar, Cleopatra, nor Lady Cicely Waynflete have any external political connexion with Puritanism. The very name of Cleopatra suggests at once a tragedy of Circe, with the horrible difference that whereas the ancient myth rightly represents Circe as turning heroes into hogs, the modern romantic convention would represent her as turning hogs into heroes. Shakespeare's Antony and Cleopatra must needs be as intolerable to the true Puritan as it is vaguely distressing to the ordinary healthy citizen, because, after giving a faithful picture of the soldier broken down by debauchery, and the typical wanton in whose arms such men perish, Shakespear finally strains all his huge command of rhetoric and stage pathos to give a theatrical sublimity to the wretched end of the business, and to persuade foolish spectators that the world was well lost by the twain. Such falsehood is not to be borne except by the real Cleopatras and Antonys (they are to be found in every public house) who would no doubt be glad enough to be transfigured by some poet as immortal lovers. Woe to the poet who stoops to such folly! The lot of the man who sees life truly and thinks about it romantically is Despair. How well we know the cries of that despair! Vanity of vanities, all is vanity! moans the Preacher, when life has at last taught him that Nature will not dance to his moralist-made tunes. Thackeray, scores of centuries later, was still baying the moon in the same terms. Out, out, brief candle; cries Shakespear, in his tragedy of the modern literary man as murderer and witch consulter. Surely the time is past for patience with writers who, having to choose between giving up life in despair and discarding the trumpery moral kitchen scales in which they try to weigh the universe, superstitiously stick to the scales, and spend the rest of the lives they pretend to despise in breaking men's spirits. But even in pessimism there is a choice between intellectual honesty and dishonesty. Hogarth drew the rake and the harlot without glorifying their end. Swift, accepting our system of morals and religion, delivered the inevitable verdict of that system on us through the mouth of the king of Brobdingnag, and described Man as the Yahoo, shocking his superior the horse by his every action. Strindberg, the only genuinely Shakespearean modern dramatist, shews that the female Yahoo, measured by romantic standards, is viler than her male dupe and slave. I respect these resolute tragicomedians: they are logical and faithful: they force you to face the fact that you must either accept their conclusions as valid (in which case it is cowardly to continue living) or admit that their way of judging conduct is absurd. But when your Shakespears and Thackerays huddle up the matter at the end by killing somebody and covering your eyes with the undertaker's handkerchief, duly onioned with some pathetic phrase, as The flight of angels sing thee to thy rest, or Adsum, or the like, I have no respect for them at all: such maudlin tricks may impose on tea-drunkards, not on me.

Besides, I have a technical objection to making sexual infatuation a tragic theme. Experience proves that it is only effective in the comic spirit. We can bear to see Mrs. Quickly pawning her plate for love of Falstaff, but not Antony running away from the battle of Actium for love of Cleopatra. Let realism have its demonstration, comedy its criticism, or even bawdry its horse-laugh at the expense of sexual infatuation, it if must; but to ask us to subject our souls to its ruinous glamor, to worship it, deify it, and imply that it alone makes our life worth living, is nothing but folly gone mad erotically—a thing compared to which Falstaff's unbeglamored drinking and drabbing is respectable and right-minded. Whoever, then, expects to find Cleopatra a Circe and Caesar a hog in these pages, had better lay down my book and be spared a disappointment.

In Caesar, I have used another character with which Shakespear has been beforehand. But Shakespear, who knew human weakness so well, never knew human strength of the Caesarian type. His Caesar is an admitted failure: his Lear is a masterpiece. The tragedy of disillusion and doubt, of the agonized struggle for a foothold on the quicksand made by an acute observation striving to verify its vain attribution of morality and respectability to Nature, of the faithless will and the keen eyes that the faithless will is too weak to blind: all this will give you a Hamlet or a Macbeth, and win you great applause from literary gentlemen; but it will not give you a Julius Caesar. Caesar was not in Shakespear, nor in the epoch, now fast waning, which he inaugurated. It cost Shakespear no pang to write Caesar down for the merely technical purpose of writing Brutus up. And what a Brutus! A perfect Girondin, mirrored in Shakespear's art two hundred years before the real thing came to maturity and talked and stalked and had its head duly cut off by the coarser Antonys and Octaviuses of its time, who at least knew the difference between life and rhetoric.

It will be said that these remarks can bear no other construction than an offer of my Caesar to the public as an improvement on Shakespear's. And in fact, that is their precise purport. But here let me give a friendly warning to those scribes who have so often exclaimed against my criticisms of Shakespear as blasphemies against a hitherto unquestioned Perfection and Infallibility. Such criticisms are no more new than the creed of my Diabolonian Puritan or my revival of the humors of Cool as a Cucumber. Too much surprise at them betrays an acquaintance with Shakespear criticism so limited as not to include even the prefaces of Dr. Johnson and the utterances of Napoleon. I have merely repeated in the dialect of my own time and in the light of its philosophy what they said in the dialect and light of theirs. Do not be misled by the Shakespear fanciers who, ever since his own time, have delighted in his plays just as they might have delighted in a particular breed of pigeons if they had never learnt to read. His genuine critics, from Ben Jonson to Mr. Frank Harris, have always kept as far on this side idolatry as I.

As to our ordinary uncritical citizens, they have been slowly trudging forward these three centuries to the point which Shakespear reached at a bound in Elizabeth's time. Today most of them have arrived there or thereabouts, with the result that his plays are at last beginning to be performed as he wrote them; and the long line of disgraceful farces, melodramas, and stage pageants which actor-managers, from Garrick and Cibber to our own contemporaries, have hacked out of his plays as peasants have hacked huts out of the Coliseum, are beginning to vanish from the stage. It is a significant fact that the mutilators of Shakespear, who never could be persuaded that Shakespear knew his business better than they, have ever been the most fanatical of his worshippers. The late Augustin Daly thought no price too extravagant for an addition to his collection of Shakespear relics; but in arranging Shakespear's plays for the stage, he proceeded on the assumption that Shakespear was a botcher and he an artist. I am far too good a Shakespearean ever to forgive Henry Irving for producing a version of *King Lear* so mutilated that the numerous critics who had never read the play could not follow the story of Gloster. Both these idolators of the Bard must have thought Forbes Robertson mad because he restored Fortinbras to the stage and played as much of Hamlet as there was time for instead of as little. And the instant success of the experiment probably altered their minds no further than to make them think the public mad. Mr. Benson actually gives the play complete at two sittings, causing the aforesaid numerous critics to remark with naive surprise that Polonius is a complete and interesting character. It was the age of gross ignorance of Shakespear and incapacity for his works that produced the revival of serious indiscriminate eulogies with which we are familiar. It was the attention to those works that coincided with the movement for giving genuine instead of spurious and silly representations of his plays. So much for Bardolatry!

It does not follow, however, that the right to criticize Shakespear involves the power of writing better plays. And in fact—do not be surprised at my modesty—I do not profess to write better plays. The writing of practicable stage plays does not present an infinite scope to human talent; and the playwrights who magnify its difficulties are humbugs. The summit of their art has been attained again and again. No man will ever write a better tragedy than *Lear*, a better comedy than *Le Festin de Pierre* or *Peer Gynt*, a better opera than *Don Giovanni*, a better music drama than *The Niblung's Ring*, or, for the matter of that, better fashionable plays and melodramas than are now being turned out by writers whom nobody dreams of mocking with the word immortal. It is the philosophy, the outlook on life, that changes, not the craft of the playwright. A generation that is thoroughly moralized and patriotized, that conceives virtuous indignation as spiritually nutritious, that murders the murderer and robs the thief, that grovels before all sorts of ideals, social, military, ecclesiastical, royal and divine, may be, from my point of view, steeped in error; but it need not want for as good plays as the hand of man can produce. Only, those plays will be neither written nor relished by men in whose philosophy guilt and innocence, and consequently revenge and idolatry, have no meaning. Such men must rewrite all the old plays in terms of their own philosophy; and that is why, as Stuart-Glennie has pointed out, there can be no new drama without a new philosophy. To which I may add that there can be no Shakespear or Goethe without one either, nor two Shakespears in one philosophic epoch, since, as I have said, the first great comer in that epoch reaps the whole harvest and reduces those who come after to the rank of mere gleaners, or, worse than that, fools who go laboriously through all the motions of the reaper and binder in an empty field. What is the use of writing plays or painting frescoes if you have nothing more to say or shew than was said and shewn by Shakespear, Michael Angelo, and Raphael? If these had not seen things differently, for better or worse, from the dramatic poets of the Townley mysteries, or from Giotto, they could not have produced their works: no, not though their skill of pen and hand had been double what it was. After them there was no need (and *need* alone nerves men to face the persecution in the teeth of which new art is brought to birth) to redo the already done, until in due time, when their philosophy wore itself out, a new race of nineteenth century poets and critics, from Byron to William Morris, began, first to speak coldly of Shakespear and Raphael, and then to rediscover, in the medieval art which these Renascence masters had superseded, certain forgotten elements which were germinating again for the new harvest. What is more, they began to discover that the technical skill of the masters was by no means superlative. Indeed, I defy anyone to prove that the great epoch makers in fine art have owed their position to their technical skill. It is true that when we search for examples of a prodigious command of language and of graphic line, we can think of nobody better than Shakespear and Michael Angelo. But both of them laid their arts waste for centuries by leading later artists to seek greatness in copying their technique. The technique was acquired, refined on, and elaborated over and over again; but the supremacy of the two great exemplars remained undisputed. As a matter of easily observable fact, every generation produces men of extraordinary special faculty, artistic, mathematical and linguistic, who for lack of new ideas, or indeed of any ideas worth mentioning, achieve no distinction outside music halls and class rooms, although they can do things easily that the great epoch makers did clumsily or not at all. The contempt of the academic pedant for the original artist is often founded on a genuine superiority of technical knowledge and aptitude: he is sometimes a better anatomical draughtsman than Raphael, a better hand at triple counterpoint than Beethoven, a better versifier than Byron. Nay, this is true not merely of pedants, but of men who have produced works of art of some note. If technical facility were the secret of greatness in art, Swinburne would be greater than Browning and Byron rolled into on, Stevenson greater than Scott or Dickens, Mendelssohn than Wagner, Maclise than Madox Brown. Besides, new ideas make their technique as water makes its channel; and the technician without ideas is as useless as the canal constructor without water, though he may do very skilfully what the Mississippi does very rudely. To clinch the argument, you have only to observe that the epoch maker himself has generally begun working professionally before his new ideas have mastered him sufficiently to insist on constant expression by his art. In such cases you are compelled to admit that if he had by chance died earlier, his greatness would have remained unachieved, although his technical qualifications would have been well enough established. The early imitative works of great men are usually conspicuously inferior to the best works of their forerunners. Imagine Wagner dying after composing Rienzi, or Shelley after Zastrozzi! Would any competent critic then have rated Wagner's technical aptitude as high as

Rossini's, Spontini's, or Meyerbeer's; or Shelley's as high as Moore's? Turn the problem another way: does anyone suppose that if Shakespear had conceived Goethe's or Ibsen's ideas, he would have expressed them any worse than Goethe or Ibsen? Human faculty being what it is, is it likely that in our time any advance, except in external conditions, will take place in the arts of expression sufficient to enable an author, without making himself ridiculous, to undertake to say what he has to say better than Homer or Shakespear? But the humblest author, and much more a rather arrogant one like myself, may profess to have something to say by this time that neither Homer nor Shakespear said. And the playgoer may reasonably ask to have historical events and persons presented to him in the light of his own time, even though Homer and Shakespear have already shewn them in the light of their time. For example, Homer presented Achilles and Ajax as heroes to the world in the *Iliad*. In due time came Shakespear, who said, virtually: I really cannot accept this spoilt child and this brawny fool as great men merely because Homer flattered them in playing to the Greek gallery. Consequently we have, in Troilus and Cressida, the verdict of Shakespear's epoch (our own) on the pair. This did not in the least involve any pretence on Shakespear's part to be a greater poet than Homer.

When Shakespear in turn came to deal with Henry V and Julius Caesar, he did so according to his own essentially knightly conception of a great statesman-commander. But in the XIX century comes the German historian Mommsen, who also takes Caesar for his hero, and explains the immense difference in scope between the perfect knight Vercingetorix and his great conqueror Julius Caesar. In this country, Carlyle, with his vein of peasant inspiration, apprehended the sort of greatness that places the true hero of history so far beyond the mere *preux chevalier,* whose fanatical personal honor, gallantry, and self-sacrifice, are founded on a passion for death born of inability to bear the weight of a life that will not grant ideal conditions to the liver. This one ray of perception became Carlyle's whole stock-in-trade; and it sufficed to make a literary master of him. In due time, when Mommsen is an old man, and Carlyle dead, come I and dramatize the by-this-time familiar distinction in *Arms and the Man*, with its comedic conflict between the knightly Bulgarian and the Mommsenite Swiss captain. Whereupon a great many playgoers who have not yet read Cervantes, much less Mommsen and Carlyle, raise a shriek of concern for their knightly ideal as if nobody had ever questioned its sufficiency since the middle ages. Let them thank me for educating them so far. And let them allow me to set forth Caesar in the same modern light, taking the platform from Shakespear as he from Homer, and with no thought of pretending to express the Mommsenite view of Caesar any better than Shakespear expressed a view which was not even Plutarchian, and must, I fear, be referred to the tradition in stage conquerors established by Marlowe's Tamerlane as much as to the chivalrous conception of heroism dramatized in *Henry V*.

For my own part I can avouch that such powers of invention, humor and stage ingenuity as I have been able to exercise in *Plays Pleasant and Unpleasant*, and these *Three Plays for Puritans*, availed me not at all until I saw the old facts in a new light. Technically, I do not find myself able to proceed otherwise than as former playwrights have done. True, my plays have the latest mechanical improvements: the action is not carried on by impossible soliloquys and asides; and my people get on and off the stage without requiring four doors to a room which in real life would have only one. But my stories are the old stories; my characters are the familiar harlequin and columbine, clown and pantaloon (note the harlequin's leap in the third act of *Caesar and Cleopatra*); my stage tricks and suspenses and thrills and jests are the ones in vogue when I was a boy, by which time my grandfather was tired of them. To the young people who make their acquaintance for the first time in my plays, they may be as novel as Cyrano's nose to those who have never seen Punch; whilst to older playgoers the unexpectedness of my attempt to substitute natural history for conventional ethics and romantic logic may so transfigure the eternal stage puppets and their inevitable dilemmas as to make their identification impossible for the moment. If so, so much the better for me: I shall perhaps enjoy a few years of immortality. But the whirligig of time will soon bring my audiences to my own point of view; and then the next Shakespear that comes along will turn these petty tentatives of mine into masterpieces final for their epoch. By that time my twentieth century characteristics will pass unnoticed as a matter of course, whilst the eighteenth century artificiality that marks the work of every literary Irishman of my generation will seem antiquated and silly. It is a dangerous thing to be hailed at once, as a few rash admirers have hailed me, as above all things original: what the world calls originality is only an unaccustomed method of tickling it. Meyerbeer seemed prodigiously original to the Parisians when he first burst on them. Today, he is only the crow who followed Beethoven's plough. I am a crow who have followed many ploughs. No doubt I seem prodigiously clever to those who have never hopped, hungry and curious, across the fields of philosophy, politics, and art. Karl Marx said of Stuart Mill that his eminence was due to the flatness of the surrounding country. In these days of Free Schools, universal reading, cheap newspapers, and the inevitable ensuing demand for notabilities of all sorts, literary, military, political and fashionable, to write paragraphs about, that sort of eminence is within the reach of very moderate ability. Reputations are cheap nowadays. Even were they dear, it would still be impossible for any public-spirited citizen of the world to hope that his reputation might endure; for this would be to hope that the flood of general enlightenment may never rise above his miserable high-water mark. I hate to think that Shakespear has lasted 300 years, though he got no further than Koheleth the Preacher, who died many centuries before him; or that Plato, more than 2000 years old, is still ahead of our voters. We must hurry on: we must get rid of reputations: they are weeds in the soil of ignorance. Cultivate that soil, and they will flower more beautifully, but only as annuals. If this preface will at all help to get rid of mine, the writing of it will have been well worth the pains.

Fun & Games

"Awake the pert and nimble spirit of mirth."
—*A Midsummer Night's Dream*, I,1,13

TWO SHAKESPEAREAN CROSSWORD PUZZLES

by Janet Muggeridge

I

"What's in a name? That which we call a rose
By any other name would smell as sweet."
—*Romeo and Juliet*

Place the play characters listed below into the grid. (Answers on page 91.)

AENEAS, ANTONY, BAGOT, BIANCA, CATO, CLEOPATRA, COSTARD,
EMILIA, ENOBARBUS, IAGO, IRAS, KATE, LEAR, MACBETH, MALVOLIO,
MIRANDA, OPHELIA, PORTIA, ROSALIND, TITANIA, TYBALT, VIOLA

II
"A man of fire-new words . . ."
—*Love's Labour's Lost*

Each answer is a word coined by Shakespeare (or traditionally so attributed). Each clue is a synonym for that word's "present-day" meaning. (Answers on page 91.)

ACROSS
1 Mountain climber (11)
6 The academic world (7)
8 Considered beforehand (12)
9 Self-reproaches (12)
11 Not diminished or moderated (11)
12 Bamboozled (10)
13 Unfounded (8)
14 Deftly (11)

DOWN
2 Identical (17)
3 Arguing (11)
4 Demoralized (12)
5 Favorable (10)
7 Myriad (13)
9 Innumerable (9)
10 Monolithic (10)

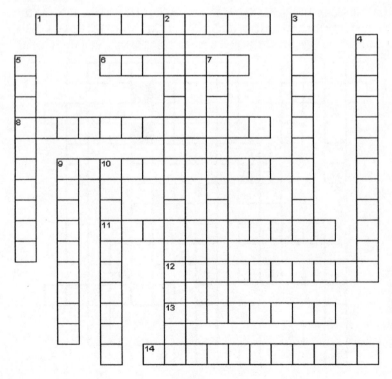

SHAKESPEAREAN QUIZZES

by Jeffrey McQuain and Stanley Malless

Comedies: Title Test

Shakespeare scholars have developed their own shorthand for identifying the plays. Following are the standard abbreviations used for the comedies. Name the titles, which are arranged in the same order used in the First Folio of 1623. (Answers on page 92.)

1. TMP	5. ERR	9. MV	13. TN
2. TGV	6. ADO	10. AYL	14. WT
3. WIV	7. LLL	11. SHR	
4. MM	8. MND	12. AWW	

Introducing Comedy

Following are the opening lines of five Shakespearean comedies. Connect these first lines to the titles of the comedies they introduce. (Answers on page 92.)

1. "If music be the food of love, play on,"
2. "Now, fair Hippolyta, our nuptial hour / Draws on apace."
3. "In delivering my son from me, I bury a second husband."
4. "Cease to persuade, my loving Proteus:"
5. "As I remember, Adam, it was upon this fashion bequeath'd me by will. . . ."

A. *The Two Gentlemen of Verona*   D. *All's Well That Ends Well*
B. *As You Like It*   E. *A Midsummer Night's Dream*
C. *Twelfth Night*

EXTRA CREDIT:
Name the characters who speak these opening lines.

Kings and Queens

Shakespeare's plays—comedy, history, and tragedy—include many kings and queens among their principal roles. The following lists contain the names of several of these ruling characters. Connect the king and queen that compose each royal couple. (Answers on page 92.)

1. Henry VI   A. Anne Bullen
2. Henry VIII   B. Isabel
3. Richard III   C. Margaret
4. Leontes   D. Anne
5. Charles VI   E. Gertrude
6. Claudius   F. Hermione

EXTRA CREDIT:
Name the plays in which these royal couples appear.

Movies and the Bard

Shakespeare's influence on motion pictures has been significant since the making of the first full-length movies. A half-dozen questions about Shakespeare's films follow. (Answers on page 93.)

1. What is the oldest surviving full-length motion picture made in America?
   A. *King Lear*   B. *Richard III*   C. *Romeo and Juliet*

2. Which Shakespeare film was first to win an Academy Award?
   A. *Hamlet*   B. *Henry V*   C. *A Midsummer Night's Dream*

3. What actress received an Oscar nomination for *Romeo and Juliet*?
   A. Claire Danes   B. Olivia Hussey   C. Norma Shearer

4. Which Shakespeare play was the first to win an Oscar for Best Picture?
   A. *Hamlet*   B. *Julius Caesar*   C. *The Tempest*

5. Which Shakespeare play was the latest to win an Oscar for Best Picture?
   A. *Hamlet*   B. *Macbeth*   C. *Othello*

6. For which Shakepeare play did Kenneth Branagh receive his first Oscar nomination?
   A. *Hamlet*   B. *Henry V*   C. *Much Ado About Nothing*

EXTRA CREDIT:
In the late 1920s, a film version of *The Taming of the Shrew* gained notoriety for a screen credit. What was that controversial credit?

SHAKESPEARE MADLIB
by Brandon Geist

Up for some silliness? Then try this Elizabethan twist on the favorite party game. Track down an unsuspecting friend, ask him or her for the words listed under the blanks, fill these in, and read aloud the literary atrocity that results.

To _____ or not to _____,—that is the _____;
    VERB   VERB   NOUN

Whether 'tis nobler in the _____ to suffer
                                 NOUN

The Slings and _____ of _____ fortune,
                PLURAL NOUN   ADJECTIVE

Or to take _____ against a sea of _____,
            PLURAL NOUN   PLURAL NOUN

And by a _____ end them. To die,—to _____—
       VERB ENDING IN -ING   VERB

No more; and by a _____ to say we end
                  VERB

The _____ and the _____ natural shocks
      NOUN   A BIG NUMBER

That the flesh is _____ to,—'tis a _____
           A PROFESSION OR STATUS   NOUN

_____ to be wish'd. To _____,—to _____,—
  ADVERB   VERB   VERB

To _____! Perchance to _____! Ay, there's the _____;
   PREVIOUS VERB   VERB   NOUN

For in that _____ of death what _____ may come
         VERB   PLURAL NOUN

When we have _____ off this _____ coil,
          PAST-TENSE VERB   ADJECTIVE

Must give us _____ . . .
         NOUN

SHAKESPEARE ON SCREEN
by Brandon Geist

To lovers of language, a silent Shakespearean film might sound about as entertaining as a silent concerto, but from 1899 to 1927, more than four hundred Shakespearean silent films were made. To the early film directors, Shakespeare was ideal for silent pictures—pretty much everyone knew the basic plotlines, so Hamlet would hold up a skull, Caesar would be stabbed, Romeo and Juliet would pine, the audience could fill in the rest.

Fortunately for all of us who'd actually like to hear the rest, sound film was invented. And as one might expect, this innovation caused Shakespeare to lose little appeal as a source for the cinema. Below is a not nearly comprehensive list of some of the more notable (or just plain eccentric) filmic (with sound) adaptations, transmutations, and outright bastardizations of the bard's work. Included are numerous examples of bizarre casting (James Cagney as Bottom?), bizarre settings (outer space, feudal Japan, high school, high school again), and in one case, a bizarre amount of nudity (anyone see *Prospero's Books?*). So browse and pick your viewing pleasure with discretion.

The Taming of the Shrew (1929), starring Douglas Fairbanks, Mary Pickford. Directed by Sam Taylor.

A Midsummer Night's Dream (1935), starring Mickey Rooney, James Cagney. Directed by Max Reinhardt and William Dieterle.

Romeo and Juliet (1935), starring Norma Shearer, Leslie Howard, John Barrymore, Basil Rathbone. Directed by George Cukor.

As You Like It (1936), starring Laurence Olivier. Directed by Paul Czinner.

Henry V (1945). Directed by Lawrence Olivier.

Macbeth (1948). Directed by Orson Welles.

Hamlet (1948). Directed by Lawrence Olivier.

Othello (1952). Directed by Orson Welles.

Julius Caesar (1953), starring Marlon Brando, James Mason. Directed by Joseph L. Mankiewicz.

Richard III (1955). Directed by Lawrence Olivier.

Forbidden Planet (1956), (based on *The Tempest*). Directed by Fred M. Wilcox.

Throne of Blood (1957), (based on *Macbeth*), starring Toshiro Mifune, Isuzu Yamada. Directed by Akira Kurosawa.

West Side Story (1961), (based on *Romeo and Juliet*), starring Natalie Wood, Richard Beymer, Russ Tamblyn, Rita Moreno. Directed by Robert Wise and Jerome Robbins.

The Bad Sleep Well (1963), (based on *Hamlet*). Directed by Akira Kurosawa.

Hamlet (1964), starring Richard Burton. Directed by Bill Colleran and John Gielgud.

The Taming of the Shrew (1966), starring Elizabeth Taylor, Richard Burton. Directed by Franco Zeffirelli

Romeo and Juliet (1968). Directed by Franco Zeffirelli.

King Lear (1970), starring Yuri Yarvet. Directed by Grigori Kozintsev.

King Lear (1971) starring Paul Scofield. Directed by Peter Brook.

Macbeth (1972). Directed by Roman Polanski.

Antony and Cleopatra (1974), starring Patrick Stewart, Ben Kingsley. Directed by Trevor Nunn and John Schoffield.

Comedy of Errors (1978), starring Judi Dench, Francesca Annis. Directed by Philip Casson and Trevor Nunn.

A Midsummer Night's Sex Comedy (1982), starring Woody Allen, Mia Farrow. Directed by Woody Allen.

King Lear (1984), starring Laurence Olivier. Directed by Michael Elliot.

Ran (1985), (based on *King Lear*), starring Tatsuya Nakadai, Mieko Harada. Directed by Akira Kurosawa.

King Lear (1987). Directed by Jean-Luc Godard.

Henry V (1989), starring Kenneth Branagh, Judi Dench, Paul Scofield. Directed by Kenneth Branagh.

Romeo and Juliet (1990), starring Francesca Annis, Vanessa Redgrave, Ben Kingsley. Directed by Armando Acosta II.

Hamlet (1990), starring Mel Gibson, Glenn Close, Helena Bonham-Carter. Directed by Franco Zeffirelli.

Prospero's Books (1991), (based on *The Tempest*). Directed by Peter Greenaway.

Rosencrantz and Guildenstern Are Dead (1991), starring Gary Oldman, Tim Roth. Directed by Tom Stoppard.

Much Ado About Nothing (1993). Directed by Kenneth Branagh.

Richard III (1996), starring Ian McKellen, Annette Bening, Maggie Smith, Robert Downey, Jr. Directed by Richard Loncraine.

William Shakespeare's Romeo and Juliet (1996), starring Leonardo DiCaprio, Claire Danes. Directed by Baz Luhrman.

Hamlet (1996), starring Kenneth Branagh, Richard Attenborough, Judi Dench, Billy Crystal, Kate Winslet. Directed by Kenneth Branagh.

Twelfth Night (1996), starring Helena Bonham-Carter, Nigel Hawthorne, Ben Kingsley. Directed by Trevor Nunn.

Looking for Richard (1996). Directed by Al Pacino.

Shakespeare in Love (1998), (loosely inspired by Cesario/Viola of *Twelfth Night Or What You Will* and *Romeo and Juliet*), starring Joseph Fiennes, Gwyneth Paltrow, Geoffrey Rush, Judi Dench. Directed by John Madden.

10 Things I Hate About You (1999), (based on *The Taming of the Shrew*), starring Julia Stiles, Heath Ledger. Directed by Gil Junger.

A Midsummer's Night's Dream (1999), starring Calista Flockhart, Michelle Pfeiffer. Directed by Michael Hoffman.

Titus (1999), starring Anthony Hopkins, Alan Cumming, Jessica Lange. Directed by Julie Taymor.

Love's Labour's Lost (2000). Directed by Kenneth Branagh.

Hamlet (2000), starring Ethan Hawke, Julia Stiles, Kyle MacLachlan. Directed by Michael Almereyda

O (2001), (based on *Othello*), starring Mekhi Phifer, Josh Hartnett, Julia Stiles. Directed by Tim Blake Nelson.

ANSWERS

I

II

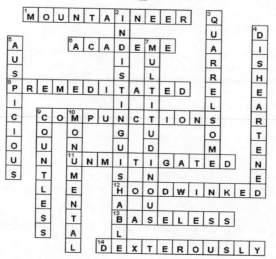

Comedies: Title Test

1. TMP = *The Tempest*
2. TGV = *The Two Gentlemen of Verona*
3. WIV = *The Merry Wives of Windsor*
4. MM = *Measure for Measure*
5. ERR = *The Comedy of Errors*
6. ADO = *Much Ado About Nothing*
7. LLL = *Love's Labour's Lost*
8. MND = *A Midsummer Night's Dream*
9. MV = *The Merchant of Venice*
10. AYL = *As You Like It*
11. SHR = *The Taming of the Shrew*
12. AWW = *All's Well That Ends Well*
13. TN = *Twelfth Night*
14. WT = *The Winter's Tale*

Introducing Comedy

1. C. Perhaps the most famous opening line of a Shakespearean comedy, these words are spoken by Duke Orsino to begin *Twelfth Night*.

2. E. Theseus says these words to his betrothed, Hippolyta, at the start of *A Midsummer Night's Dream*.

3. E. The Countess of Rossillion bemoans the departure of her son, Bertram, at the beginning of *All's Well That Ends Well*.

4. A. Valentine, one of *The Two Gentlemen of Verona*, speaks to the other, Proteus, to lead into that comedy.

5. B. Orlando starts *As You Like It* by expressing dissatisfaction with his lot to the elderly servant Adam.

Kings and Queens

1. C. Henry VI marries Margaret in *1 Henry VI*, and they both appear in the other two parts of the *Henry VI* trilogy. (Margaret is a widow in *Richard III*.)

2. A. Henry VIII divorces Katherine to marry her maid of honor, Anne Bullen, in *Henry VIII*. (The name of the new queen, who gives birth to the future Elizabeth I, is also spelled *Anne Boleyn*.)

3. D. Anne, the widowed daughter-in-law of Henry VI, is wooed and won by the title character of *Richard III*.

4. F. In *The Winter's Tale*, Hermione is the Queen to Leontes, the King of Sicilia.

5. B. Charles VI, King of France in *Henry V*, is married to Isabel.

6. E. *Hamlet* presents the royal couple of Claudius and Gertrude (although the name of Claudius is never spoken in the play.)

Movies and the Bard

1. B. Recently discovered was a 1912 five-reel production of *Richard III*; America's oldest surviving feature film runs approximately 55 minutes.

2. C. In 1935, a production of *A Midsummer Night's Dream* (featuring a young Mickey Rooney as Puck) was nominated for Best Picture and won Oscars for its cinematography by Hal Mohr and edited by Ralph Dawson.

3. C. All three actresses have played Juliet, but it was Norma Shearer who received a 1936 nomination for *Romeo and Juliet*; she lost the Oscar to Luise Rainer, star of *The Great Ziegfeld*.

4. A. Laurence Olivier's 1948 production of *Hamlet* was the first Shakespeare film to win the Oscar for Best Picture.

5. A. A trick question—no other Shakespeare film has ever won the Oscar for Best Picture.

6. B. In 1989, Kenneth Branagh received nominations as actor and director for *Henry V* (the film won for its costume design by Phyllis Dalton).

EXTRA CREDIT:
Mary Pickford and Douglas Fairbanks starred in the 1929 film version of *The Taming of the Shrew*. That movie, directed by Sam Taylor, displays an infamous writing credit: "By William Shakespeare, with additional dialogue by Sam Taylor."

Acknowledgments

Leonard Barkan, "What Did Shakespeare Read?" from *The Cambridge Companion to Shakespeare*, edited by Margreta de Grazia and Stanley Wells. Copyright © 2001 by Cambridge University Press. Reprinted with the permission of Cambridge University Pres.

Harold Bloom, "Shakespeare's Universalism" from *Shakespeare: The Invention of the Human*. Copyright © 1998 by Harold Bloom. Reprinted with the permission of Riverhead Books, an imprint of Penguin Putnam Inc.

Norrie Epstein, "No-Holds Bard: A Glossary of Sexual Slang" and "Was Shakespeare Gay?" from *The Friendly Shakespeare*. Copyright © 1993 by Norrie Epstein. Reprinted with the permission of Viking Penguin, a division of Penguin Putnam Inc.

Brandon Geist, "Shakespeare Madlib" and "Shakespeare on Screen." Both reprinted by the permission of the author.

Bernard Levin, excerpt from *Enthusiasms*. Copyright © 1983 by Bernard Levin. Reprinted with the permission of Crown Publishers, a division of Random House, Inc.

Jeffrey McQuain and Stanley Malless, excerpt from "Introduction" of *Coined by Shakespeare*. Copyright © 1998 by Jeffrey McQuain and Stanley Malless. Reprinted with the permission of Merriam-Webster, Inc., www.Merriam-Webster.com.

Jeffrey McQuain and Stanley Malless, Quizzes 3, 9, 11, and 13 from *Coined by Shakespeare*. Copyright © 1998 by Jeffrey McQuain and Stanley Malless. Reprinted with the permission of Merriam-Webster, Inc., www.Merriam-Webster.com.

Margaret Miner and Hugh Rawson, "Shakespeare and His Works" from *A Dictionary of Quotations from Shakespeare*, edited by Margaret Miner and Hugh Rawson. Copyright © 1992 by Hugh Rawson and Margaret Miner. Reprinted with the permission of Dutton Signet, a division of Penguin Putnam Inc.

Janet Muggeridge, The Bard of Avon, Crosswords 2 and 6 from www.wordplayfsnet.co.uk. Copyright © by Janet Muggeridge. Reprinted by permission.

Joseph Sobran, excerpt from "The Authorship Debate" from *Alias Shakespeare: Solving the Greatest Literary Mystery of All Time* (New York: Free Press, 1997). Copyright © 1997 by Joseph Sobran. Reprinted with the permission of Writers' Representatives, Inc.